P9-CRP-890

My Tuscany

LORENZA DE' MEDICI

My Tuscany

RECIPES CUISINE LANDSCAPE

PHOTOGRAPHY BY

JOHN FERRO SIMS

DUNCAN BAIRD PUBLISHERS

LONDON

My Tuscany
Lorenza de' Medici

First published in the United Kingdom and Ireland in 2003 by
Duncan Baird Publishers Ltd
Sixth Floor
Castle House
75–76 Wells Street
London W1T 3QH

Conceived, created and designed by Duncan Baird Publishers.

Managing Editor: Judy Barratt
Editors: Lucy Latchmore and Diana Loxley
Designers: Dan Sturges and Rachel Cross
Picture Research: Julia Brown
Commissioned maps: Garry Walton

British Library Cataloguing-in-Publication Data:
A CIP record for this book is available from the British Library.

ISBN: 1-904292-66-6

10 9 8 7 6 5 4 3 2 1

Typeset in Garamond and Helvetica
Colour reproduction by Color & Print Gallery Sdn Bhd, Malaysia
Printed in China by Imago

PUBLISHER'S NOTES
Although all reasonable care has been taken in the preparation of this book, neither the Publisher nor the Author can accept any liability for any consequences arising from the use thereof, or the information contained therein.

Recipe conversions are approximate.

Vin Santo
Del Chianti

CONTENTS

Foreword 8

Siena and its province **14**
Pinzimonio (Raw vegetables dipped in olive oil) 19
Ribollita (Twice boiled bean soup) 25
Polpettine rifatte (Meatballs in tomato sauce) 30
Rapini all'aglio (Broccoli raab with garlic) 31
Panello con l'uva (Flatbread with grapes) 39

Florence and its province **42**
Schiacciata al ramerino (Flatbread with rosemary) 47
Malfatti di spinaci (Spinach and *ricotta* dumplings) 51
Arista arrosto morto (Roasted pork loin) 56
Patate in tegame (Braised potatoes) 57
Zuccotto (Florentine pudding) 65

Arezzo and its province **68**
Frittura di salvia (Fried sage leaves) 73
Pappardelle sulla lepre (*Pappardelle* with hare sauce) 77
Scottiglia (Mixed braised meats) 82
Fagioli all'uccelletto (Beans in tomato sauce) 83
Castagnaccio (Chestnut cake) 87

Grosseto and its province **88**
Crostini di fegatini (Chicken-liver toast) 93
Acquacotta maremmana (Vegetable egg soup) 97
Cinghiale in agrodolce (Wild boar in sweet and sour sauce) 100
Teste di funghi in cartoccio (Mushroom caps cooked in foil) 101
Cenci (Fried pastry) 107

Massa-Carrara, Lucca, Pistoia, Prato and their provinces **108**
Bruschetta al lardo di Colonnata (Toasted bread with lard) 113
Minestra di farro (Emmer soup) 119
Seppie in zimino (Cuttlefish with spinach) 124
Carciofi al funghetto (Sautéed artichokes) 125
Biscotti di Prato (Almond biscuits from Prato) 131

Livorno, Pisa and their provinces **132**
Fiori di zucca ripieni d'acciughe (Zucchini flowers stuffed with anchovies) 137
Spaghetti all'astice (Spaghetti with lobster sauce) 141
Zuppa di cozze (Mussel soup) 144
Peperoni al forno (Roasted peppers) 145
Torta di mele e pinoli (Apple and pinenut cake) 151

Directory 152
Glossary 158

Acknowledgments 160

N
CARRARA
MASSA
R. Sèrchio
PISTOIA
PRATO
LUCCA
FLORENCE
LIGURIAN SEA
R. Arno
PISA
LIVORNO
AREZZO
SIENA
ISLAND OF ELBA
GROSSETO
R. Ombrone
R. Albegna
TYRRHENIAN SEA
0
20 km
0
20 miles

FOREWORD

Knowledge and appreciation of Tuscan food have developed considerably during the many years I have been writing about Italian cooking. Early in my career, several general books about Italian cooking appeared – most were written by non-Italians and had broad titles, such as *Northern Italian Cooking* and *Southern Italian Cooking*. References to Tuscany were, at best, fleeting and when they did crop up, were sometimes to be found in the wrong geographical location! Then there appeared on the market a series of books in which the cooking of Italy was more precisely divided according to the country's different regions, with chapters on the food of Piedmont, Tuscany, Sicily, and so on. These, in turn, were followed by books that were wholly dedicated to the cooking of single regions.

Although this regional approach has undoubtedly marked a major step forward in the understanding of Italian cooking, it still does not go to the heart of the tradition. While a visitor to Italy might think of particular dishes as being Venetian or Tuscan, a Tuscan would identify his or her favourite dish with the particular place or province within the region from which it originated. Thus, for Tuscans, *cacciucco*, the region's famed fish soup (see pages 134–40), is not a Tuscan dish, it is Livornese, from the port of Livorno where it originated and where, they will tell you, the best and most authentic *cacciucco* is still made. Similarly, any Tuscan eating *zuppa di farro* in a Florentine restaurant would not think of this traditional soup as Florentine but as Lucchese, from the province of Lucca where *farro*, a special grain,

is grown (see page 118). Accordingly, I have chosen to adopt a local or provincial approach in this book.

Modern Tuscany is divided into ten separate governmental provinces: Siena, Florence, Arezzo, Grosseto, Massa-Carrara, Lucca, Pistoia, Prato, Pisa and Livorno. Each of the provinces is characterized by, among other factors, its distinctive terrain: some, such as Grosseto, are marked by their mountainous landscape; others, such as Lucca, by their proximity to the sea or, as in the case of Arezzo, by their fertile valleys. Over the centuries, each of these areas has developed its own particular culinary tradition, based on local ingredients prepared by local cooks.

It is ancient wisdom – although not often sufficiently emphasized in cookery books – that a dish is only as good as the quality of its ingredients. This is particularly true of Tuscan cooking, which has its roots in the country, and is tied to the land and conditioned by the seasons. The deliciousness of any Tuscan dish depends far more on the high quality of its ingredients than on the skills of the cook. I have tried to reflect this principle in the pages which follow and have therefore focused on local food production – for this reason, this book should be considered a food book rather than a recipe book. Many of the products discussed – such as fine, extra virgin olive oil from Chianti – are now exported all over the world, so it will be possible for you to prepare most of the dishes at home. Others, such as lard from Colonnata or sheep's milk cheese from Pienza, cannot be sampled until you visit the province. Nevertheless, I still think it well worth knowing how best to enjoy them when you are here. Many of the products can be carried home as gastronomic souvenirs.

I have concentrated throughout on describing a few of the most traditional ways of preparing these local products, rather than giving long and often meaningless lists of provincial dishes. The recipes I have chosen are all authentic and classic. There is, of course, a place in

the kitchen for innovation and for the adaptation of a tradition – but that is for other books. My approach here is strictly "back to roots".

The recipes are placed throughout each section wherever they best illustrate how to use a certain food, and I have selected them so that, together, they make up a complete menu typical of the particular province of Tuscany being discussed. There are five recipes for each section: an *antipasto*, a first course, a main course, a side dish and a dessert. It is my hope that you will derive satisfaction and enjoyment from preparing these dishes in the kitchen and that they will give you, your family and your guests immense pleasure when you sit down together at the table to sample them.

SIENA

AND ITS PROVINCE

The province of Siena forms the geographic centre of Tuscany and is a region of astonishing beauty, both natural and human-made. To the north lie the rolling hills of Upper Chianti, where olive groves, wooded areas and vineyards are interspersed with medieval castles and ancient, stone farmhouses. It is here that Tuscany's finest olive oil is produced – a precious green-gold liquid, aromatic and fruity. To the south is the undulating terrain of the Crete Senesi, whose fertile soil provides rich pastures for flocks of sheep. The local *pecorino* cheese, made from ewe's milk, is one of Tuscany's most prestigious products. And the province's splendid capital, the city of Siena, still specializes in the production of medieval confections – in particular, the sweet and pungent *panforte*.

It was, I remember, a particularly hot and humid August afternoon when I arrived in Tuscany on my first visit to Badia a Coltibuono, the country home and wine estate of my husband's family. We had set out that morning by car from our home in Milan. The journey took us south through the valley of the Po River, with its vast fields of rice and corn, into the fertile region of Emilia-Romagna, past its capital city, Bologna, then over the crest of the Apennine mountains, down into the valley of the Arno River and, finally, into the sweltering heat of Florence. Soon we began to ascend the high hills of Chianti through vineyards and olive groves to a fresh and cooling altitude of some 600 metres (200ft).

Suddenly, in the midst of a vast forest, Coltibuono came into view, a splendid, sprawling structure of cut stone, austere but not unfriendly, overlooking the valley of the Arno River to the north and the province of Siena to the south. Coltibuono began its life in the year 1000CE as a Benedictine Abbey and became our family farm

Continued on page 21 ☞

These vineyards, which dominate the landscape around San Gimignano, produce a delicious local white wine called Vernaccia di San Gimignano.

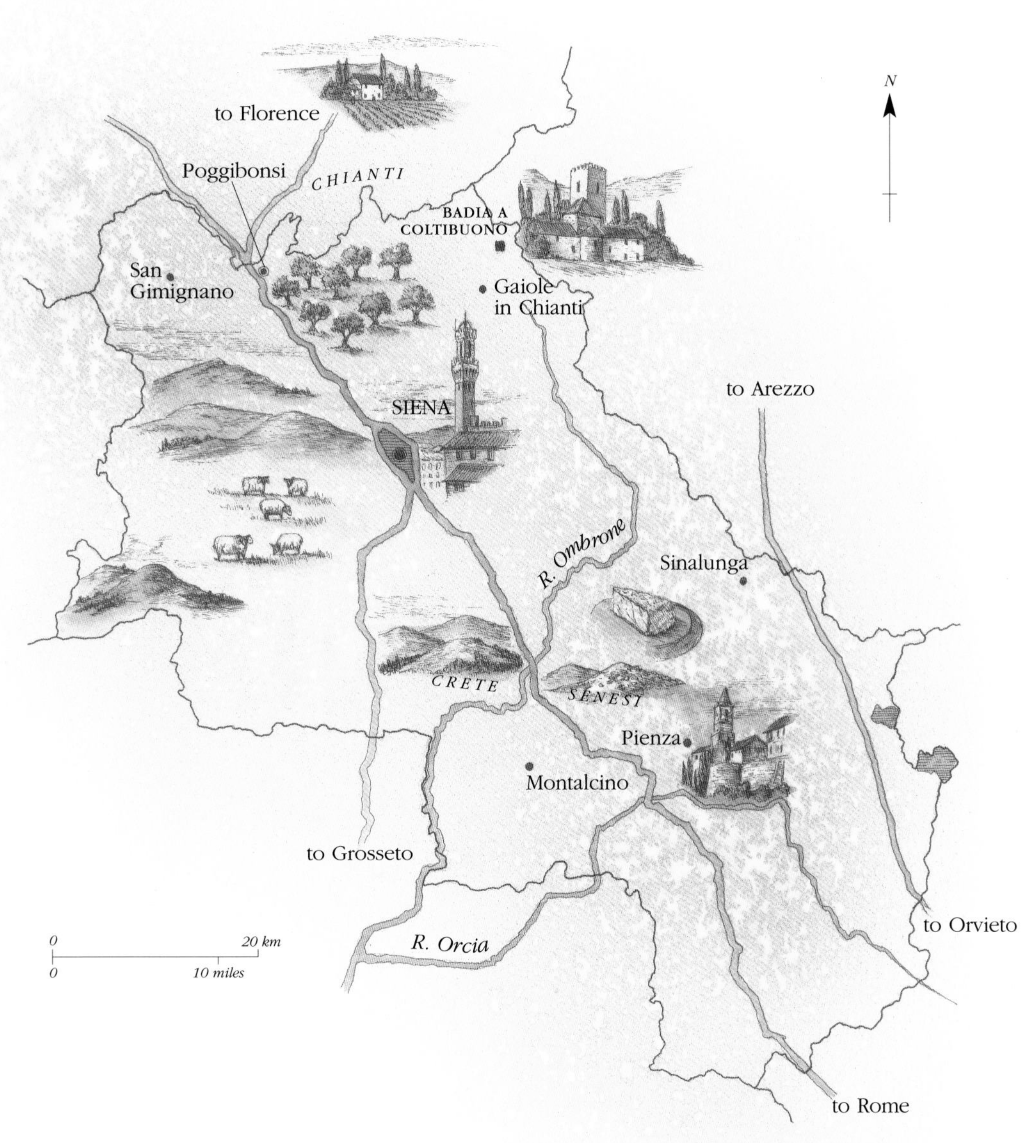
N
to Florence
Poggibonsi
CHIANTI
BADIA A
COLTIBUONO
San
Gimignano
Gaiole
in Chianti
SIENA
to Arezzo
R. Ombrone
Sinalunga
CRETE
SENESI
Pienza
Montalcino
to Grosseto
to Orvieto
R. Orcia
0
20 km
0
10 miles
to Rome

PINZIMONIO

Raw vegetables dipped in olive oil

This is a colourful and tasty way to begin a light summer lunch. The word pinzimonio *describes the tangy taste of full-flavoured, extra virgin olive oil, the principal ingredient of the dish. In Tuscany, we like to savour the taste of our olive oil, pure and unadulterated, so we season it simply with salt and pepper. The selection of vegetables is up to you: fennel, celery, carrots, radishes and bell peppers are among those most often used.*

2 carrots
2 white celery hearts
2 fennel bulbs
240ml/8fl oz/1 cup extra virgin olive oil
salt and pepper

1. Peel the carrots and slice them vertically into slender sticks.
2. Trim the celery hearts, separate the stalks and slice them thinly.
3. Clean the fennel, discard the tough outer leaves and slice the bulbs vertically.
4. Wash all the vegetables well and arrange them in a bowl at the centre of the table.
5. Pour the oil into individual bowls, add salt and pepper to taste and place in front of each diner.

Serves 6

ABOVE: Olive groves and woods alternate with vines on hills crested with cypress trees in the Chianti area, where much of Tuscany's best wine and olive oil is produced. OPPOSITE: Jars of olive oil flavoured with bay leaves and wild fennel flowers.

and country home eight centuries later. Today it is our year-round residence.

Our primary product – both on the estate and throughout the area generally – is wine, with olive oil a close second. Many other parts of Tuscany and several regions of Italy also produce fine olive oils, but over the years I have come to esteem the oil of Upper Chianti as the absolute best. This judgment is, of course, subjective. When olive oil is a staple of your diet, as it is for every Tuscan, your local oil becomes like mother's milk – only your own is perfectly satisfying.

There are also objective or technical reasons that contribute to the superior taste of the olive oils from this region. The altitude at which the olive trees are cultivated is, for example, significant. Olive groves are planted on hillsides at altitudes ranging from 350 to 550 metres (1,150–1,800ft) – exceptionally high for what is, after all, a Mediterranean fruit tree. As a result, the olives never develop to glossy black and plump maturity, as they do

at lower elevations, and are picked when they are still lean and partially green. These under-ripe olives give the oil its characteristic cold-green colour, fresh aroma and particularly pungent and fruity, full-flavoured taste, in contrast to the pale yellow appearance, fatty odour and bland taste of certain other oils.

The excellence of these olives is also due to the manner in which they are harvested. At lower elevations in more southern parts of Tuscany and the

Continued on page 24 ☞

OPPOSITE: In Siena's Upper Chianti area, olives are traditionally harvested by hand during the month of November. Pickers climb up into the trees on wooden ladders and comb the olives off the branches into baskets.

ABOVE: Once the freshly picked olives have been pressed for oil, the fresh oil is traditionally stored in terracotta urns called orci *(centre top). Today, however, these ancient vessels are gradually being replaced by stainless-steel containers.*

DRAGONCELLO

Dragoncello is the Tuscan name for tarragon, a herb usually associated with French cuisine and virtually unknown in Italian cooking, except in Siena where a local variety of the plant exists. The Siennese make *salsa verde*, green sauce, with *dragoncello* instead of with flat-leaf parsley, which is used in the rest of Italy. It is combined with minced garlic, anchovies, capers, vinegar, either hard-boiled egg yolks or breadcrumbs and extra virgin olive oil. The sauce is served with *bollito misto* (mixed boiled meats) and with fish.

Mediterranean, olives are left to mature until they are so heavy with oil that they drop from their branches onto nets spread below the trees. They bruise easily during this process, causing the oil to smell and taste like rank, stale fat. In Upper Chianti, the olives are picked by hand and are not permitted to mature to a state of heavy oiliness. They are left to ripen on the tree as long as possible and are picked before they are nipped by the first frost. Around mid-November, with their bare, hardened hands or with a special kind of comb, farmers rake the olives from the branches into a basket slung over their shoulders. Time-consuming and costly though this method is, it eliminates the risk of rancidity and ensures that the olives arrive at the mill in prime condition.

The manner in which the olives are milled and pressed also affects the quality of the oil. Traditionally, farmers in Upper Chianti take their olives to mills that employ the "cold press" method. Several variations on this centuries-old procedure exist, but the essential factor is that no heat or chemicals are applied to the olives to extract their oil – this ensures that their natural flavours and nutritional qualities remain intact. The flesh of the fruit, but not the stone, is crushed under immense granite stones. The resulting mash is spread on fibrous mats

RIBOLLITA

Twice boiled bean soup

This soup encapsulates all that is dear to the heart of the Tuscan cook: it is savoury, nourishing and puts leftovers to good use. Traditionally, stale bread was added to leftover soup which was then reheated. Nowadays, it is most often made and served on the same day.

240g/8oz/2 cups dry white *cannellini* beans
900g/2lb black cabbage, sliced
120ml/4fl oz/½ cup extra virgin olive oil
2 red onions, chopped
3 celery stalks, diced
3 carrots, diced
1 litre/2 pints/4 cups water
3 thyme sprigs
12 slices stale, coarse, country bread
3 garlic cloves, crushed
salt and pepper

1. Cover the beans with water, bring them slowly to the boil and cook on a very low heat until tender (about 2 hours).
2. Cook the cabbage with 3 tablespoons of the oil in a covered pot, on a low heat, for about 10 minutes. Add the onions, celery and carrots and continue cooking very slowly for a further 10 minutes.
3. Pass half the beans through a food processor and add to the soup, along with the rest of the (whole) beans, the water in which they were cooked and the clean water. Add the thyme, and salt and pepper to taste. Cover and cook on a low heat for about 1 hour.
4. Brush the bread with the garlic and arrange half of it in a soup tureen; add half of the soup, the rest of the bread, and then the remainder of the soup. Allow to cool completely. Bring back to the boil and serve. Add a tablespoon of the rest of the oil to each soup bowl.

Serves 6

and then pressed. The oil extracted from this process contains a watery substance that is eliminated, usually by means of a centrifuge.

Oil from hand-picked olives cultivated at the high altitude of Upper Chianti and pressed in this traditional manner is relatively rare and expensive, even here. It is a labour-intensive, low-yield process: 18 kilos (26lb) of oil produced from 100 kilos (220lb) of olives would be considered an excellent yield. Pickers prefer to be paid in kind rather than in cash – an indication of how greatly the oil is valued.

Olive oil holds pride of place on the Tuscan table. It is poured generously over slices of grilled country bread, fresh greens, cooked and raw vegetables (see recipe, page 19), some cuts of meat, and is even drizzled on *pecorino*, the local sheep's milk cheese (see pages 29–37). In the kitchen, it is the foundation of all cooking. High quality olive oil is capable of completely transforming commonplace meals, while inferior oil can wreck the most carefully prepared dishes.

I am often asked how to choose a fine oil from the relatively large choice now available in shops. My advice is to go to a reliable merchant who has a good selection and ask to be pointed to the oils of Upper Chianti. The standard label indications are not definitive guarantees of quality, although they can be helpful. According to Italian law, "extra virgin" means the oil has less than one per cent acidity (all fine oils will have even less). "Cold

OPPOSITE: Rounds of mature pecorino *– a prestigious Tuscan table cheese. ABOVE: Artisans making* pecorino *by pressing ewe's milk curds into circular moulds and rubbing them with salt.*

pressed" and "from the first pressing" are important quality factors. "Produced and bottled by", followed by the name of the estate, assures you that the oil in the bottle came from the area on the label. If the estate makes fine wine as well as olive oil, the quality of the oil should also be high. Select bottles from two different producers and see which one tastes better to you.

One of the most delicious olive oils is *olio nuovo* or "new oil" – it is difficult to find, and can often only be bought from the producer or from the *frantoio*, the local mill. Olive oil is considered "new" within the first three months of its pressing, from late November to February: it is bright chlorophyll green in colour, has a rich vegetal aroma and a piquant, peppery aftertaste – characteristics that soften with time. *Olio nuovo* is one of those brief, seasonal, gastronomic experiences we all await come winter. The traditional and best way to savour this oil is on the classic *fettunta*, literally, an "oiled" slice of grilled bread which is rubbed with garlic before the new oil is poured over it.

In all of Tuscany only one kind of cheese is produced that can be considered both traditional and local. The reason is that there are practically no cows. Once you cross over the Apennine mountains from northern Italy into Tuscany, you leave behind the extensive pastures required for grazing cattle and enter into hills and dales where small flocks of sheep dot the landscape.

The Italian word for a ewe is *pecora*, and the cheese made from her milk is called *pecorino*. Several areas in Tuscany produce *pecorino*, but I think the best

Continued on page 33 ☞

A view of the hills and vineyards that surround the medieval town of Montalcino, where one of world's most celebrated wines – Brunello di Montalcino – is produced.

POLPETTINE RIFATTE

Meatballs in tomato sauce

This dish, which is never eaten with pasta, is typically Tuscan and a family favourite. Romolo, our cook at Coltibuono, prepared it in the manner described here for three generations of my family. Rifatte *means "remade" and refers to recooking the meatballs in tomato sauce.*

600g/20oz chopped lean beef
2 handfuls fresh, coarse country breadcrumbs, soaked in milk for about 5 minutes and squeezed dry
240g/8oz fresh sausagemeat
1 tablespoon finely chopped onion
1 tablespoon finely chopped fresh flat-leaf parsley
2 eggs
flour for dusting
240g/8oz/1 cup dry breadcrumbs
1 litre/2 pints/4 cups oil for deep-frying meatballs
3 tablespoons extra virgin olive oil
3 garlic cloves, chopped
480g/16fl oz/2 cups tomato purée
salt and pepper

1. In a bowl, mix the beef with the soft breadcrumbs, sausagemeat, onion, parsley and egg until well-blended. Add salt and pepper to taste. Dust your hand with flour and form meatballs the size of extra-large eggs. Coat them well in the dry breadcrumbs.
2. Heat the oil in a pan and deep-fry the meatballs until golden (about 10 minutes). Allow them to cool.
3. Fry the garlic in extra virgin olive oil until barely golden; add the tomato purée and cook for a few minutes. Add salt and pepper and the meatballs. Cover and cook for about 10 minutes on a low heat, turning them delicately a couple of times. If the tomato sauce becomes too thick, add a little water.
4. Arrange the meatballs on a platter and serve. *Rapini all'aglio* (see opposite) is a wonderful accompaniment to this dish.

Serves 6

RAPINI ALL'AGLIO

Broccoli raab with garlic

Tuscans like greens with a slightly bitter flavour, and broccoli raab, or rapini, *is a firm favourite. The greens are prepared very simply: sautéed in extra virgin olive oil with a little garlic. This dish makes a perfect accompaniment to the meatballs in tomato sauce (see opposite).*

1 kilo/2lb broccoli raab
3 garlic cloves, chopped
3 tablespoons extra virgin olive oil
salt and pepper

1. Bring a pot of water to the boil, add the broccoli raab and blanch for a couple of minutes. Drain.
2. Fry the garlic in the oil on a low heat, until barely golden. Add the broccoli raab, cover and cook for about 5 more minutes, stirring gently a couple of times. Add salt and pepper to taste.
3. Arrange on a platter and serve.

Serves 6

comes from a unique stretch of land called the Crete Senesi, which extends south of Siena for some 500 square kilometres (200 square miles) to the hilltop town of Pienza. The area consists of undulating clay hills (*crete* means clay) created millions of years ago from deposits left by the receding sea. No vines or olive trees grow in this part of Tuscany – it is a strangely lunar-like landscape. As you drive along the crest of hills, a solitary farmhouse occasionally comes into view, and in the further distance, a single cypress atop a knoll. In spring, a blanket of blue-green grass interwoven with wild herbs and flowers covers the humid, lime-rich soil of the Crete, producing perfect pasture for the flocks of sheep that graze there, giving their milk its distinctive flavour.

This breed of sheep is local and increasingly scarce. Sheep today are mostly bred for their meat and no longer produce a quality and quantity of milk suitable for making cheese. *Pecorino* production in the Crete has largely remained a cottage industry, using centuries-old artisan methods. Traditionally, the curds are separated from the whey by means of a vegetable rennet, obtained from the

OPPOSITE: Sheep grazing on the hills of the Val d'Orcia, whose fragrant pastures give their cheese its unique taste.

ABOVE: Stacks of pecorino *in varying stages of maturity; the rounds with dark rinds have been rubbed with ash for flavour.*

flowers of wild cardoons or artichokes. The curds are then pressed by hand into cylindrical forms until all the remaining liquid has drained away. They are rubbed with salt and then left to dry on wooden shelves in a dark and well-ventilated room, where they are turned every three or four days.

Pecorino toscano is ready to eat within a week, although it is usually left to mature for anything between three and six months before going to market. Very young, "fresh" *pecorino* has a milky colour and aroma, a soft, creamy texture and a refined, aromatic sweetness. With age, the crust turns from straw yellow to golden brown, the texture dries, the taste sharpens and its aromatic flavour becomes more decisive.

Considered a table cheese, *pecorino toscano* is too delicious and precious to be used for grating or cooking, unlike its more forceful and widely available counterpart from Rome, *pecorino romano.* In early spring, when the first batch of *pecorino* is ready to eat, I serve it with the

PICI

Pasta of every kind is eaten in Tuscany today, but only two types are local in origin and can be considered typically Tuscan: *pappardelle* (see page 77) and *pici*, in some places called *pinci*, the pasta of Siena.

Pici are a kind of homemade spaghetti, that are relatively thick and short. They are made with flour and water, no eggs. The soft, springy dough is rolled by hand into noodles about 20 to 25 centimetres (8 to 10in) long and 0.3 centimetres (1/8in) thick (thinner rather than thicker is better). Classically, *pici* are dressed with rich sauces such as a thick meat *ragù*, tomato and sausage, and fresh *porcini* mushrooms. They have their origin in family kitchens and have been popular in the area's country *trattorie*, but it is only recently that they have been produced commercially, dried and made available in packages.

season's fresh broad beans, dressed with extra virgin olive oil. A wedge of seasoned, somewhat piquant *pecorino*, combined with a sweet, juicy pear is an ideal way to end a meal – the contrasting yet complementary textures and tastes make it one of those gastronomic marriages made in heaven.

Artisan *pecorino* production creates two special by-products. The first, *raveggiolo*, is simply the curds that are lifted intact from the whey, once the milk has curdled. They are put in small, individual moulds to drain before being turned out to eat. *Raveggiolo* is classified as a soft, full-fat cheese. It is always eaten fresh, simply seasoned with salt, usually as an *antipasto*, and has a very delicate taste. I like to serve it on a bed of peppery wild *rucola* (rocket).

Ricotta is the second by-product of *pecorino*. During cheese making, when the whey is being pressed out of the curds, it is collected in a container and immediately afterward made into *ricotta*. The process is simple. The leftover whey still retains protein; when the liquid is brought to the boil, the protein coagulates and comes to the surface as *ricotta*. It is then skimmed off and placed in a perforated mould to drain. *Ricotta* remains lumpy and moist and must be eaten fresh.

Many traditional Tuscan recipes use *ricotta*. The most classic dish is large *ravioli* – pasta parcels stuffed with spinach and *ricotta*, and dressed simply with butter and fresh sage leaves. *Ricotta* is also a popular dessert ingredient – it is the key ingredient in *ricotta* cake, which is one of the most delicious and delicate of the Italian desserts. A favourite way to eat *ricotta* in my family is to cream it with a fork, mix in a couple of cups of finely ground coffee, and sprinkle it with sugar. Fresh fruit purées or jams can be substituted for the coffee.

Genuine *pecorino toscano* is difficult to find outside the areas of its production, which is all the more reason to search it out and bring back home a round or two. The best place to shop for it in the Crete Senesi is in the

ABOVE: Panforte, *a dense, sweet Siennese cake made with almonds, candied fruit and a unique blend of spices. The original medieval recipe included black pepper and a pinch of chilli, and is called* panpepato *(pepper cake).*
OPPOSITE: The procession that precedes the twice-yearly Palio horse race in Siena's splendid Piazza del Campo.

tiny and exquisite Renaissance town of Pienza, built by a native son, Silvio Piccolomini, after he became Pope Pius II. In a document written in the mid-fifteenth century, he wrote that the *pecorino* from his hometown was "the best of the best". Locally, this is considered an infallible papal decree. The road winding up to Pienza displays signs indicating farms that sell *pecorino*, while the narrow streets of the town itself are lined with food shops, each with its own selection of the artisan-made speciality. Let your eyes and nose be your guides. I would buy from the generous merchant who offers you a tasting of his or her fine cheese, especially if they pour a glass of local red wine to go along with it.

From the hill above my home at Coltibuono, I can see the cityscape of Siena 30 kilometres (18 miles) in the distance, unchanged since medieval times. Three magnificent structures rise above the rose-coloured rooftops, dominating the horizon: the slender and elegant stone tower of the town hall and the black-and-white striped marble tower and white dome of the cathedral.

These were built during the High Middle Ages, when Siena was at the peak of its prestige between the mid-twelfth century, when it became an independent republic, and the mid-fourteenth century, when the black plague practically decimated its population. It owed its wealth and power to its merchant bankers, who were active throughout all of Europe and beyond.

Among other ambitious enterprises, the citizens of Siena financed a number of crusades to the Holy Land. Those returning from these trips to the Middle East brought back with them various exotic spices, which they offered to Siena's many monasteries in thanksgiving for their safe return. The monks and nuns used these

Continued on page 40 ☞

PANELLO CON L'UVA

Flatbread with grapes

This bread, traditionally baked and served at harvest time in Chianti, contains fresh red grapes – it is this ingredient that gives it its distinctive character. The baker in my town of Gaiole in Chianti in the province of Siena turns it out in large sheets and sells it by weight. It is a favourite snack of local school children, who line up to buy a slice while it is still hot from the oven. I bake it in a round pan and serve it as dessert.

30g/1oz fresh yeast
240ml/8fl oz/1 cup lukewarm water
360g/12oz/3 cups wholewheat flour
flour for dusting
30g/1oz unsalted butter
180g/6oz fat, juicy red grapes
3 tablespoons caster sugar

1. Preheat the oven to 200°C/400°F.
2. Dissolve the yeast in the water for about 10 minutes. Place in a bowl with the flour and start mixing with a fork in a circular motion until the water is absorbed and a dough is formed. Form a ball with the dough and transfer it to a floured surface: work it with the heels of the hands for a few minutes, until smooth. Reform a ball, place in a floured bowl and cover tightly with clingfilm. Allow to rise until double in size (the rising time depends on room temperature).
3. Butter and dust a round tart pan of about 30cm/12in diameter with flour. On a floured surface, roll the dough to fit the pan. Cover with a cloth and allow to rise for 10 more minutes. Arrange the grapes on top of the dough, sprinkle with the sugar and cook for about 30 minutes, or until golden and well risen. Serve at room temperature.

Serves 6

FLORENCE

AND ITS PROVINCE

I find it reassuring that the capital of Tuscany, Italy's most agricultural region, is also the country's most artistically gifted city: good food nourishes the human spirit as well as the body. Florence, the cradle of the Renaissance, produces great cooking as well as great art. Its culinary achievements are based on high-quality products from the countryside, which are magnificently displayed in the capital's several markets.

Despite the city's cultural sophistication, its cooking is simple, even rustic: *trippa alla fiorentina*, tripe cooked with tomatoes, is a Florentine favourite; pork from tenderly raised local pigs is another unforgettable traditional dish; and artisan producers turn out a variety of mouthwatering savoury processed pork products, including delicious sausages and salami.

In Florence, as would befit Tuscany's capital, you can find all the foods for which the region is famous. Begin your gastronomic tour at the city's food markets. Three, in particular, are well worth a visit. The biggest, busiest and most fascinating is the Mercato Centrale, located in the neighbourhood in which the Medici lived, down the street from their palace and parish church, San Lorenzo – the first church in Florence to be built in the Renaissance style.

The market is housed in a huge, mid-nineteenth-century two-storey building of cast-iron and glass, which takes up an entire city block. The streets surrounding it remind me of a Middle Eastern *souk*, chock-a-block with stalls selling bargain-priced clothes. In the midst of the bustling crowds and mountains of merchandise the entrance to the food market is almost hidden from view.

Once through the door, you enter a wondrous world, a maze of aisles lined with hundreds of specialized stalls selling salami, meat, poultry, game, fish, cheese, pasta, bread, baked goods, olives, candied fruit and nuts. I always explore the fish section first, led on by the fresh scent of the sea that wafts from it. The catch of the day might include a bounteous array of clams, mussels, scallops, shrimps, squid and octopus, as well as sea bass, tuna, swordfish and numerous other fish – many from the waters off the Tuscan coast.

Continued on page 49 ☞

Florence's cathedral cupola, designed and constructed in 1436 by Brunelleschi (one of the pioneers of early-Renaissance architecture in Italy) with the aid of machines that Brunelleschi invented expressly for the project.

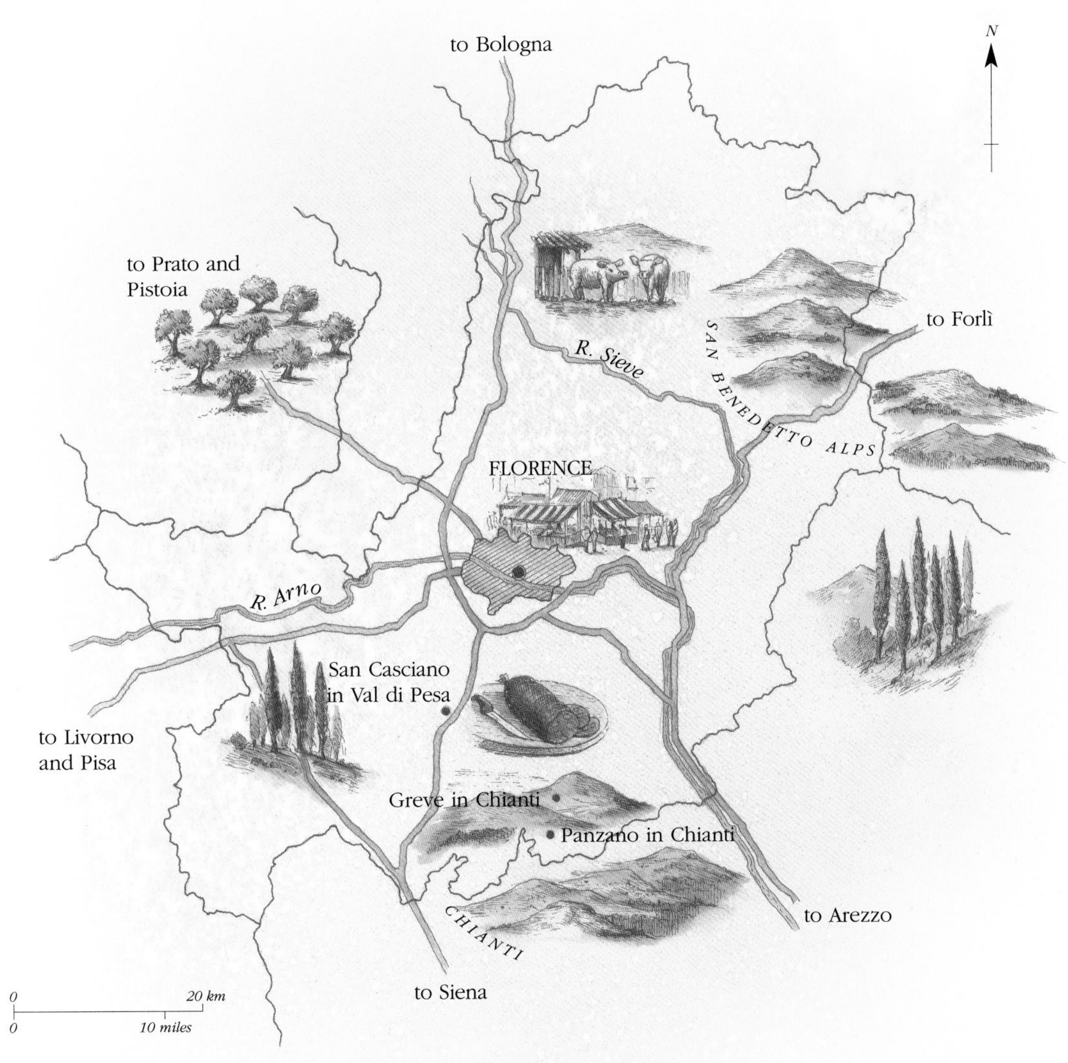
to Bologna
N
to Prato and
Pistoia
to Forlì
R. Sieve
SAN BENEDETTO ALPS
FLORENCE
R. Arno
San Casciano
in Val di Pesa
to Livorno
and Pisa
Greve in Chianti
Panzano in Chianti
to Arezzo
CHIANTI
to Siena
0
20 km
0
10 miles

SCHIACCIATA AL RAMERINO

Flatbread with rosemary

Schiacciata*, or "squashed", is the name Florentines give to their version of flatbread. Basic* schiacciata alla fiorentina *is sprinkled with salt, brushed with olive oil and baked until golden. It is often topped with a variety of seasonal ingredients, including tomatoes, sweet peppers and zucchini. This recipe with rosemary is the most classic of all. Cut into finger-sized slices, it is ideal served with an* aperitivo*, such as a glass of wine.*

30g/1oz fresh yeast

240g/8fl oz/1 cup lukewarm water

360g/12oz/3 cups plain flour

flour for dusting

60ml/2fl oz/¼ cup extra virgin olive oil

3 rosemary sprigs

salt

1. Preheat the oven to 200°C/400°F.
2. Dissolve the yeast in the water for about 10 minutes. Place in a bowl with the flour and mix with a fork in a circular motion until the water is absorbed and a dough is formed. Form a ball with the dough and transfer it to a floured surface: work it with the heel of the hands for a few minutes, until smooth. Reform into a ball, place in a floured bowl and cover tightly with clingfilm. Allow to rise until double in size (the rising time depends on the room temperature).
3. Brush a round tart pan of about 30cm/12in diameter with oil. On a floured surface, roll the dough to fit the pan and arrange it in the pan. Cover with a cloth and allow to rise for 10 more minutes. Sprinkle with the rosemary, salt to taste and the rest of the oil. Cook for about 30 minutes or until golden on top. Allow to cool slightly and serve.

Serves 6

DILL (ANETO)
MENTA
TIMO
CRESCIONE
SELVATICO
SALVASTRELLA
RUCOLA
SELVATICA
E TANTI ALTRI
SPUGNINA

My favourite area is the top floor, which boasts magnificent, sprawling displays of fruit and vegetables. Here, vendors vie with each other not only for the best offer, but also for the most attractive presentation. Depending on the season, there are piles of white fennel, purple artichokes, red, yellow and green peppers, mounds of broad beans and pyramids of blood oranges. In spring, some stalls feature baskets of wild greens, and in autumn, different varieties of mushrooms.

Before leaving the building, stop for a boiled-beef sandwich at Nerbone, a Florentine institution. The beef is sliced hot on the spot. Regulars like their bread roll moistened in the warm broth in which the beef was cooked. When in Florence, do as the Florentines do, and wash it down with a glass of Chianti.

On the other side of town, still within the city centre, is the market of Sant'Ambrogio, which is not as large as the Mercato Centrale, but has an added attraction: one section of the outdoor stalls surrounding the market building is reserved for the farmers from the countryside. They sell greens, vegetables and fruit, all fresh from the garden and at the peak of their season. Increasingly, much of the produce is labelled as organically grown.

For a taste of a small neighbourhood market, cross the Arno River by the Santa Trinità bridge and

OPPOSITE: An abundance of fresh greens and vegetables can be found in Florence's fine produce markets.

ABOVE: An antipasto *platter of marinaded tripe, as served at Florence's renowned Cibreo restaurant.*

(One of the city's most popular tripe vendors sets his stall on the street just outside the restaurant.)

proceed a couple of blocks to the tree-lined Piazza di Santo Spirito. There, with the splendidly simple façade of the Renaissance church of Santo Spirito as their backdrop, are a scattering of stalls selling a selection of fine produce. One of the attractions here is watching the locals engaged in animated repartee with their favourite vendors. You need not understand Italian – facial expressions and body language say it all.

You cannot walk around Florence for long, at least if you take the small back streets, without coming upon the most characteristic of all Florentine gastronomic traditions. What first attracts your attention is the crowd of locals swarming around a steaming stainless-steel stand. What some are waiting to buy and what others are already enjoying are boiled-tripe sandwiches. These Florentine street gourmets, young and old, construction workers and fashionably dressed women, are all fans of this immensely popular food, which is fragrant, succulent, tender and delicately flavoured.

Tripe, *trippa* in Italian, is the lining of the stomach of ruminants such as cows, oxen, sheep and deer. Ruminants have a four-chambered stomach, three "pre-stomachs", plus the actual stomach itself. Each part is edible, producing four types of tripe. The first and largest is called the rumen, the second is called the reticulum, the third is the omasum and the fourth, the true stomach, is called the abomasum.

The culinary culture of every country seems to have its preferred type of tripe to which it has given a popular name. The French choose the first, the rumen, which they call *gras-double*. It is flat and smooth with two distinct sides, hence the "double" in its name. It has the most delicate flavour of the four. Most Italian main-course recipes use the reticulum, because it is the most tender. In English it is called honeycomb tripe, because of its appearance. In Italian it is named *cuffia*, a bonnet or bathing cap. San Bernadino of Siena, a popular fourteenth-century preacher, chastised the women of his day

MALFATTI DI SPINACI

Spinach and ricotta *dumplings*

Spinach paired with ricotta *is a classic Florentine combination. It is popularly used as a filling for* ravioli *or, without the pasta wrapping, as the basis for* malfatti – *spinach and* ricotta *dumplings.* Malfatti *means "badly made" and describes the crude, unrefined shape of the dumplings.*

1 kilo/2lb fresh spinach, with stems
480g/1lb *ricotta* cheese
120g/4oz/1 cup freshly grated parmesan cheese
1 egg, large
large pinch of grated nutmeg
240g/8oz/2 cups plain flour
90g/3oz unsalted butter, melted
salt and pepper

1. Bring a pot of water to the boil, add the spinach and cook for a couple of minutes, until wilted. Drain, allow to cool and squeeze well in a cloth.
2. Chop the cooked spinach finely and place in a bowl. Add the *ricotta*, half the parmesan, the egg, nutmeg and half the flour. Mix until well blended. Add salt and pepper.
3. Dust your working surface and your hands with flour. Form sausages with the mixture, about 2.5cm/1in thick, and roll in the flour. Cut them into 2.5cm/1in pieces and roll in floured hands to form ovals.
4. Bring a large pot of water to the boil. Cook the dumplings in it until they rise to the surface. Drain with a slotted spoon and arrange on a warmed platter. Sprinkle with the rest of the parmesan, pour the melted butter on top and serve immediately.

Serves 6

for their vanity in wearing frilly bonnets that, he claimed, looked "like pieces of tripe".

Florentines are crazy about the fourth type of tripe, which is discarded by most other cuisines. They call it *lampredotto*, and this is what you will find them snacking on as they stand around the tripe vendors' stalls. They slice it hot from the pot, add salt and pepper and arrange it in a crunchy roll. If the customer asks for it *bagnato*, "wet", which most of them do, they dip half the roll into the warm cooking broth.

Preparing tripe for cooking is a lengthy process, and these specialized tripe vendors, *trippai*, have been a feature of Florentine life for hundreds of years. According to a chronicle of life in sixteenth-century Florence, *trippai* in the neighbourhood of San Frediano gave their left-over broth to the local poor who would use it to dip their bread or flavour their soup. Some stalls have remained in the same location for generations. Unfortunately, other *trippai* have gone the way of many of the city's local artisans and have disappeared from the street scene. Those remaining have formed a confraternity called the *Consorzio Ambulanti Trippai* (the Consortium of Itinerant Tripe Vendors), to promote their collective interests. They come together once a year in the historic Piazza Strozzi for a convention entitled "*Civiltà della Trippa*", "Tripe Civilization".

In the evening, on their way home from work, Florentines often stop and buy tripe to take away for dinner. They will use it to make one of their most traditional dishes, *trippa alla fiorentina*. The classic

The medieval hamlet of Montefioralle above Greve in Chianti. This area of Florence is home to two of the region's finest butchers, who produce excellent pork products, sausages, several types of local salami, and Tuscan prosciutto.

recipe calls for a mixture of two types of tripe, smooth and honeycomb. It is cut into narrow strips and cooked in olive oil with chopped onion, celery and carrot. After about 10 minutes, peeled tomatoes are added, with salt and pepper to taste, and the mixture is cooked for a further 20 minutes. Its consistency should remain chewy but not rubbery. At the finish you stir in a generous portion of grated parmesan. This hugely popular dish has many variations – some cooks add garlic, chilli and white wine – but the traditional recipe remains the best.

In Florentine folklore, tripe has been called "*la signora della cucina povera*", a difficult phrase to translate but its sense can be rendered as "the noble lady of the commoner's table"; the pig has been referred to as "*il re della tavola*", "the king of the table", and depicted in popular Tuscan art sporting a crown and sceptre. Another laudatory epithet, referring specifically to processed pork products, such as salami, was "*le delizie del divin porcello*", "the delicacies of the divine pig".

The pig achieved its royal, even divine, status in Tuscany – a region lacking sufficient pastureland for the raising of herds of cattle. It was the farm animal that brought most economic and gastronomic benefit to the family and, until quite recently, every Tuscan farm raised a "family pig" (some households continue the tradition). This was usually a female – whose flesh is considered sweeter and more tender – and normally the runt of a litter, the one that would have fetched least money at market. It was spoiled and fattened on acorns, pumpkins, chestnuts and tasty bits and pieces from the family table.

Continued on page 59 ☞

OPPOSITE ABOVE: A Norcineria *is a pork butcher's shop.* Norcini *(travelling butchers originally from Norcia, in Umbria) would go as far as Florence to process the local pigs into salami and* prosciutti. *OPPOSITE BELOW: Roasted* porchetta.

NORCINERIA
Falorni

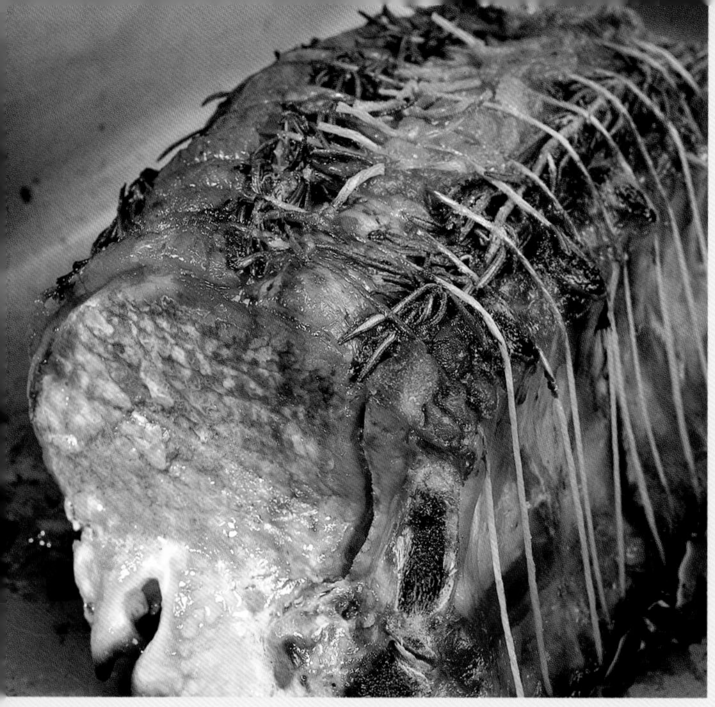

ARISTA ARROSTO MORTO

Roasted pork loin

In Tuscany, meat is often spit-roasted. When it is cooked in a pan, the method is called morto, *"dead", referring to the fact that the meat lies there, instead of revolving. This recipe sometimes includes rosemary, but I much prefer it with fennel, the classic Tuscan seasoning for roast pork.*

1 tablespoon fennel seeds
3 garlic cloves, finely chopped
1½ kilos/3lb pork loin on the bone
3 tablespoons extra virgin olive oil
60g/2oz unsalted butter
120ml/4fl oz/½ cup dry white wine
salt and pepper

1. Preheat the oven to 170°C/325°F.
2. Mix the fennel seeds, the garlic, and salt and pepper to taste. Make cuts into the meat with the point of a knife and fill with the mixture.
3. Heat the oil and butter in an oval pot on a high heat. Add the meat and cook for about 10 minutes uncovered, until golden, turning from time to time. Cover, place in the oven and cook for about 2 hours, adding a little water occasionally to keep the bottom moistened. Uncover and cook for 30 minutes more, until dark brown.
4. Arrange the meat on a serving platter. Deglaze the cooking juices with the wine, pour over the meat and serve immediately.

Serves 6

PATATE IN TEGAME

Braised potatoes

This is a traditional way to prepare potatoes in the Tuscan home and the result is wonderful. The method is simple and quick but requires a few minutes' careful attention. Instead of adding water at the end, a little tomato sauce can be used – just enough to lightly colour the potatoes.

1 kilo/2lb roasting potatoes
120ml/4fl oz/½ cup extra virgin olive oil
2 rosemary sprigs
salt and pepper

1. Peel and dice the potatoes and place them with the oil in a large non-stick pan. Add salt and pepper, and the rosemary, and cook, stirring gently, for about 10 minutes.
2. Add a little water, cover and cook until tender (about 10 minutes more).
3. Arrange on a platter and serve.

Serves 6

ABOVE LEFT: At Tuscan fairs and markets, vendors sell porchetta, *an entire roasted pig, seasoned with a mixture of rosemary, garlic and salt. ABOVE RIGHT: Wild fennel growing up to six feet tall in a Tuscan field. The feathery leaves, tiny yellow flowers and tasty white bulbs of fennel are all used in Tuscan cooking, particularly to season pork and fish.*

Then, during the cold days of winter, it would be "sacrificed" for the communal table. Every part of the animal, from the head up to, but not including, the tail, was processed and used to replenish the larder with nourishing, tasty food for the coming year.

The most famous Florentine pork dish is *arista di maiale*. Food historians disagree over how it got its name, but the recipe is ancient. Some say *arista* is simply an antiquated and altered form of the word *arrosto*, meaning roast, and cite a medieval text which speaks of someone having "*mandato un arista al forno*", "put a roast in the oven". Pellegrino Artusi, the greatest Italian cookbook writer of the nineteenth century, who lived in Florence, has a better story to tell. In 1450, an international conference of bishops was called in Florence to resolve differences between the Roman and Greek Catholic communities. The prelates were served roast loin of Tuscan pork *alla fiorentina*, which meant, in this case, cooked with garlic and rosemary. A group of Greek bishops thought it so tasty they proclaimed it "*Aristos!*", "The best!", and the name has stuck.

Out in the Florentine countryside, the pork dish that reigns supreme is *porchetta*, an entire roast pig, weighing an average of 50 kilos (110lb). More than simply a dish for a meal, it is an event in itself, and is usually sold at local festivities and markets. The preparation and cooking of *porchetta* is a major task undertaken only by a specialized *porchettaio* or by certain butchers who have the necessary equipment.

First, the pig's organs are removed and then it is washed, shaved and deboned. Its skin is left intact but slashed all over to prevent it from bursting during cooking. The cavity left by the bone is filled with a special mixture of seasonings, including rosemary, garlic and lots of salt. In some parts of Tuscany, wild fennel is added. The pork is then tied up and roasted on a spit or in a hot wood-burning brick oven. Depending on its weight, it can take up to ten hours to achieve the desired results. The flesh should be moist and the skin – my favourite part – crispy, crunchy and brown.

At festivals, you can buy *porchetta* from the vendor's stall by the slice, asking for white or dark meat, or, if you prefer, a combination of the two. It usually comes in a delicious crunchy roll and, according to taste, will include some of the seasoning – most Tuscans like a generous heap of it. At weekly village markets, housewives will often take home a few slices of *porchetta* and serve it cold for supper.

The province of Florence is famous for its processed pork products and, happily, the ancient Tuscan tradition whereby local country butchers make their own is still very much alive. These products include *prosciutto, soppressata* or "head cheese" (a large, marbled salami made from pig's head with spices and lemon peel), fresh sausages and various salami. Tuscan *prosciutto* is more salty (Tuscans would say more tasty), redder in colour and richer in flavour than the more widely known and sweeter Parma ham. It combines perfectly with saltless Tuscan country bread. High-quality *prosciutto* and salami cannot be produced just anywhere: they need to hang in a well-ventilated room for at least eight months. The atmosphere of the surrounding area is critical – it must be neither too dry nor too humid. The air of the Florentine Chianti hills is ideal, as the finished products clearly attest.

Two types of salami are typical of Tuscany. *Salame toscano* is characterized by the black peppercorns and large cubes of fat that stud the ground-pork

After it has been cured, Tuscan prosciutto *(formed from a pig's hind thighs) is hung to age in a well-ventilated room for at least eight months. Neither too dry nor too humid, the climate of the Tuscan hills is ideal for ageing* prosciutto.

mixture; it is composed of approximately 75 per cent lean meat and 25 per cent fat. Another local speciality, *finocchiona*, from the Italian word for fennel, is a large, coarse-grained salami flavoured with wild fennel seeds. A selection of processed pork products is served in Tuscan restaurants as an *antipasto*. At home, they are more commonly enjoyed as a *merenda*, a mid-morning or late afternoon snack. Accompanied by bread, cheese and a bottle of Chianti, they make the perfect picnic.

If you are travelling through the Florentine countryside, I know of at least two places worth a detour for some serious salami tasting. Under the arcade of Greve in Chianti's charming piazza, about half an hour's drive south of Florence, is the Antica Macelleria Falorni. More a gastronomic institution than a butcher's shop, it has been here for almost 200 years, run by the same family, and in recent times has expanded greatly. The first room is a traditional Tuscan butcher's shop, selling the highest quality beef, pork, lamb, poultry, wild boar and other game. On display in the two adjoining rooms are an amazing array of their tasty homemade specialities: *prosciutto*, cured and smoked bacon, pâtés, a variety of salami – all of these products are also made from wild boar. The delicacies are available in small, vacuum packed containers, so you can bring home a souvenir. On Saturdays, two *porchetta* vendors set up shop at the market held in the piazza, presenting an irresistible chance to taste another local speciality.

A few minutes' drive further up the Florentine Chianti road in the town of Panzano, you arrive at what

Lines of stately cypress trees are a common sight in Tuscany, providing windshields for crops and creating the elegant perspective imitated in Renaissance paintings. Together with the grape vine and olive tree, the cypress is a symbol of Tuscany.

ALLA FIORENTINA

An Italian culinary term which means "cooked in the manner of Florence", although its sense varies according to what is being cooked.The French use the same phrase, "à la florentine", in a different sense, to denote a specific method of food preparation, involving spinach and often Mornay sauce – a rich béchamel.

The origin of this French culinary connection between Florence and spinach goes back to Caterina de Medici, who travelled from Florence to France in 1533 to become the wife of Henri II. It is thought that while in Paris she popularized the method of combining spinach – a favourite Florentine vegetable – with other foods.

has become a place of pilgrimage for Tuscan and other carnivorous gastronomes. It is the Antica Macelleria Cecchini, a small shop run by a larger-than-life butcher. Despite his youth, Dario Cecchini has already become something of a legend in the food world: his reputation is based on his superior raw and prepared meats as well as on his personality. This is no place to do your shopping in a hurry. You might be present while Dario is in the midst of reciting a Canto from Dante's *Divine Comedy*, greeting long-lost friends or explaining how to cook one of his special dishes. He will offer you plenty to taste while you wait: a glass of Chianti from a flask, a piece of *pecorino*, a slice of his incomparably delicious *finocchiona*, fennel sausage, accompanied by bread from the wood-burning oven of the local bakery.

FOLLOWING PAGE: A view through vines of San Gimignano, a town rich in Gothic architecture. It is also one of the best-preserved Italian medieval towns, with city walls, gates and 14 out of its original 72 old towers still intact.

ZUCCOTTO

Florentine pudding

This classic Florentine dessert belongs to the category of creamy Italian confections known as semifreddo, *or "half-chilled" – served cold, not frozen, they are firm on the outside but remain soft inside. The word* zucca *means "pumpkin" (hard on the outside and soft inside).*

- 60g/2oz almonds, peeled, toasted and chopped
- 60g/2oz hazelnuts, peeled, toasted and chopped
- 60g/2oz candied orange peel, diced
- 60g/2oz chocolate coffee beans
- 60g/2oz bittersweet chocolate
- 900g/2lb *ricotta* cheese
- 120g/4oz/1 cup caster sugar
- 210g/7oz sponge fingers
- 120ml/4fl oz/½ cup Vin Santo

1. In a bowl, mix the almonds, hazelnuts, orange peel and chocolate coffee beans.
2. Melt the bittersweet chocolate by placing it on a heatproof plate over a pan of simmering water. Combine the melted chocolate with half the *ricotta*, half the nut mixture and half the sugar, and mix well.
3. In a separate bowl, mix the other half of the *ricotta* with the remaining nut mixture and sugar.
4. Line the inside of a round, 21cm/8in diameter bowl with greaseproof paper and line with the sponge fingers. Brush them with the Vin Santo and press down well. Cover with the chocolate *ricotta* mixture, level, and then add the "white" *ricotta* mixture. Level again, and cover with the rest of the sponge fingers. Brush with the remaining Vin Santo. Refrigerate for a minimum of 6 hours and a maximum of 24 hours.
5. Invert on a platter, remove the paper and serve.

Serves 8 to 10

AREZZO

AND ITS PROVINCE

Steep hills, high mountains and fertile valleys fed by Apennine streams characterize this breathtakingly beautiful eastern area of Tuscany. The valley of Val di Chiana provides rich grazing land for the local and highly prestigious breed of cattle, the Chianina. A succulent T-bone steak from prime Chianina beef constitutes an authentic *bistecca alla fiorentina* – a dish celebrated throughout Tuscany. Also indigenous to this region is a superior variety of white bean, a traditional Tuscan staple, the *zolfino*, which thrives in its native soil in the Apennine foothills of Arezzo. Home cooks and restaurant chefs alike favour local fare on their menus. Among these dishes are hare cooked in a sauce to dress the local pasta (*pappardelle*) and meats accompanied by the fine produce of the area.

Of Tuscany's ten provinces, Arezzo, located in the region's eastern sector, is the most rustic and rural and is blessed with outstanding natural beauty. The high mountains of its Casentino area are cloaked with ancient forests of pine, beech, oak and chestnut. From my bedroom window at Coltibuono, I can see them in the far distance, burning bright red and yellow in autumn; in winter the mountains' highest peaks are brilliant white with the season's first snow.

The great medieval mystic, reformer and lover of nature, Francis of Assisi, chose this remote area of Tuscany to build his hermitage and monastery, La Verna. The great Michelangelo and the renowned Renaissance painter Piero della Francesca were born here – the latter in Sansepolcro, not far from the provincial capital, Arezzo, whose church of San Francesco

The imposing 13th-century castle of Poppi stands guard above the Arno Valley. It is one of the most important and well-preserved medieval monuments in the entire Casentino area, having always been used as the residence of the local political or administrative power; today it is the seat of local government – the Commune of Poppi.

N
MONTE FALTERONA
to Cesena
CASENTINO
to Florence
La Verna
PRATOMAGNO
Caprese
VALDARNO
Lake Montedóglio
Sansepolcro
R. Arno
AREZZO
to Perugia
Can. Maestro Chiana
VAL DI CHIANA
0 10 km
0 10 miles
to Orvieto

contains his masterpiece, one of the world's greatest fresco cycles, *The Legend of the Holy Cross*, which has recently been restored.

The Arno River has its source high on the slopes of Monte Falterona. It flows down the hills of the Casentino into the Valdarno, the Valley of the Arno, through Florence and Pisa, where it finally joins the sea. In the fertile soil of the valley floor some of Tuscany's finest produce is grown. An adjoining valley, the Val di Chiana, whose river is fed from these same Apennine streams, provides rich pastureland for a local and prestigious breed of cattle called the Chianina. These beautiful white creatures, with their massive shoulders and a characteristic hump on their backs, are examples of the world's oldest and largest breeds of cattle, weighing in at several thousand pounds.

The Chianina are indigenous to the Val di Chiana, which lies at the heart of ancient Etruria. It was here that the peace-loving Etruscans founded the first civilization in what was to become Tuscany, centuries before they were overcome by Roman expansion from the south and "barbarian" invasions from the north. As testified in the drawings and sculptures they left behind, the Etruscans used Chianina as beasts of burden. When I first came to Tuscany as a young woman, they could still be seen pulling ploughs in the fields and vineyards.

The Chianina were always relatively few in number and were traditionally raised on small farms in a region in which there is limited space for grazing. With the arrival of the tractor, their numbers decreased even further. A decade or so ago, the breed was verging on extinction. An association was formed to protect them, and as a result of this initiative, small and select herds are today raised locally, principally for their prime beef.

A characteristic of the Chianina is that they grow extremely rapidly. The beautiful white Chianina oxen that are sometimes seen in local harvest parades and folkloric pageantry, have been allowed to grow to full

FRITTURA DI SALVIA

Fried sage leaves

Sage grows wild all over Italy, but it seems to be used most often in dishes from Arezzo, particularly pork dishes. I serve these sage leaves as a fingerfood with a glass of white wine. Vegetables, such as onion rings, zucchini strips and zucchini flowers, can be prepared in the same way.

30 sage leaves (wide-leaf variety)
1 egg, large
120g/4oz/1 cup plain flour
240ml/8fl oz/1 cup sparkling water
1 litre/2 pints/4 cups oil for deep-frying
salt

1. Wash and pat the sage leaves dry.
2. In a bowl, mix the egg with the flour and add the water, a little at a time, to obtain a batter. Add salt to taste.
3. Heat the oil in a deep frying pan at 170°C/325°F. Dip the leaves, a few at a time, in the batter and fry them in the oil a for few minutes, until they are barely golden.
4. Drain on kitchen paper, arrange on a dish and serve very hot.

Serves 6

ABOVE: This villa just outside Arezzo attests to the city's heyday as a Tuscan centre of culture and wealth (before Florence became the region's centre of power). OPPOSITE: The Maremmana is an indigenous Tuscan breed of cow, prized for its beef.

and impressively massive adulthood. However, the beef for Chianina steaks comes from young males under 18 months of age. It is referred to as *vitellone*, or "large veal", meat from fully grown calves – as distinct from both *vitello*, veal from a young calf, which is still being milk-fed, and *manzo*, adult beef. Because the steer is slaughtered young, its flesh is firm, without inner fat or marbling. Raised on select and organic feed, its pale red flesh is more tasty than white veal. The meat is hung for several weeks to tenderize – this lengthy period, called the *frollatura*, is possible because the meat is enclosed within a protective layer of white fat.

The most popular Chianina cut is *la fiorentina*, after the Florentine butchers who were the first to carve a rack of beef in this way. It is a T-bone steak, cut from the triangular rack of the sirloin, with the fillet attached. Traditionally, the steak is about five centimetres (2in) or, as they measure it here, "three fingers" thick, so one steak easily serves two. Restaurants charge by weight.

Today, *la fiorentina* refers as much to the method of cooking the meat as to the special cut. The classic *fiorentina* is grilled over embers of hard wood. Expert grillers sear the exterior, charring the crust very slightly, just sufficiently to seal in the juices. They turn the steak once only, after it has cooked enough to warm the interior, leaving it a rare, juicy red – *al sangue*, or bloody. The cooking time will depend, of course, on the thickness of the steak, but usually it is about three to four minutes on each side. They add salt only when the steak has finished cooking, so as not to rob it of its juices. Then they drizzle a few drops of extra virgin olive oil over the meat and add some freshly ground black pepper.

If you like your meat well done, do not order a *fiorentina* in a local restaurant. Tuscan cooks are absolutely intractable about their grilling methods. In a traditional *trattoria*, especially one that prides itself on its authentic *fiorentina*, it is virtually impossible to get a steak well done, at least the first time around. If you insist, they will reluctantly put it back on the grill – but not without displaying exasperation.

A decade or so ago, *bistecca alla fiorentina* on a restaurant menu was synonymous with Chianina. Today, genuine Chianina is rare and more often than not, your *fiorentina* will come from a more readily available and less expensive breed. However, the Chianina is gradually gaining ground, owing to the efforts of breeders and consumers who demand Chianina from butchers and restaurateurs and are willing to shop around until they find the genuine article and then pay the price. Paradoxically, modern health awareness has helped the situation: although people now eat less red meat, they want their occasional indulgence to be of the very best quality, which invariably means Chianina meat.

Bistecca is an interesting word: a relatively new addition to the Italian vocabulary, it is a corruption of the English word "beefsteak". According to linguists, it came into use in the late nineteenth century, introduced by the flourishing Anglo-American community in Florence. The original Italian word for a grilled chop is *braciola*, from brace or coals. Today, *bistecca* refers to a pork chop, *bistecca di maiale*, as well as to a beefsteak.

When a Tuscan sits down to a meal centred on an authentic *bistecca alla fiorentina*, its classic accompaniment will be a dish of white beans. Historically, beans were to Tuscany what spaghetti was to Naples – the dietary staple that gave substance to a meal, especially for a people who could hardly ever afford meat, let alone a Chianina steak. Many claim that contemporary Tuscans are such avid carnivores because for centuries they were too poor to eat meat. Instead, they ate vast quantities of protein-rich beans, "the meat of the poor". They were even characterized by their fellow countrymen as

Continued on page 80 ☞

PAPPARDELLE SULLA LEPRE

Pappardelle *with hare sauce*

Pappardelle *is a traditionally Tuscan shape of pasta usually dressed with a game sauce, such as hare or wild boar. The sauce should be rich and thick with generous pieces of meat, substantial enough to balance the considerable size of the noodles.*

3 tablespoons extra virgin olive oil
60g/2oz *pancetta*, chopped
1 medium onion, chopped
half a hare, cleaned, cut into large pieces
1 celery stalk, chopped
1 large carrot, chopped
1 handful flat-leaf parsley, chopped
1 teaspoon peppercorns
300ml/10fl oz/1¼ cups red wine
500g/1lb fresh *pappardelle*
salt

1. Fry the oil, the *pancetta* and the onion on a low heat for about 3 minutes, stirring from time to time.
2. Add the hare and sauté on a medium heat for about 10 minutes.
3. Add the celery, carrot, parsley, peppercorns and salt to taste. Cover and cook in the oven for about 30 minutes.
4. Uncover and add the wine. Cover and cook for 1 hour more. If the wine has evaporated, add a little water to keep the cooking juices topped up. Remove the hare, debone and chop the meat very coarsely. Then reheat the pieces of hare in the cooking juices to form a sauce.
5. Cook the *pappardelle* for 2 minutes in boiling, salted water. Drain and arrange on a platter. Pour half the hare sauce on top of the *pappardelle* and mix well. Pour the rest of the sauce on top and serve immediately, very hot.

Serves 6

TUSCAN BREAD

Tuscan bread is much maligned, not by Tuscans, of course, but by other Italians and foreign visitors - this is because it is unsalted, which seems to offend the taste buds of non-natives.

The Tuscan tradition of not salting bread has been variously explained. Because bread was baked in wood-burning ovens, which were difficult to fire daily, it was baked only once a week. Salt in bread draws in moisture and salted bread would become mouldy before the week was out. Unsalted bread would last until the next firing of the ovens. When it turns dry, it is moistened in a little pool of good Tuscan extra virgin olive oil; or used for Tuscan *crostini*, little slices of crusty bread spread with a tasty paste made from chopped chicken livers, anchovies and capers; or put into *ribollita*, twice boiled bean soup (see page 25); or mixed with greens and vegetables for *panzanella*, Tuscan bread salad; or cooked with tomatoes for *pappa al pomodoro*, a savoury bread pudding.

Another theory holds that as salt was highly taxed, Tuscans omitted it in their bread. This seems unlikely, as they certainly did not stint on it in their other foods. In fact, unsalted bread is the perfect balance to highly salted Tuscan food, in particular Tuscan *prosciutto*, salami and spicy meat and game sauces.

The traditional Tuscan bread, *pane toscano*, is made with white flour and turned out in big, flat loaves. The crust is crisp and thick and the inside is compact and chewy and, when freshly baked, moist. I find it is even better the next day. To palates used to salted bread, Tuscan bread at first tastes bland, but appreciation of its subtle flavour develops with time.

Pane toscano *(Tuscan bread) is baked in large, low loaves and cut to order. It is used for* crostini, *the most classic of Tuscan* antipasti, *which are usually slices of crusty bread, spread with a chicken-liver paste or simply rubbed with fresh tomatoes.*

A bowl of Zuppa alla Frantoiana – *white bean soup seasoned with onion and sage, poured over grilled country-style bread and seasoned with extra virgin olive oil. This was the traditional snack of those working in the olive mills, which are known as* frantoio *in Italian.*

mangiafagioli, bean-eaters, with the witty implication that, as you become what you eat, this explains why Tuscans are so full of beans.

Be that as it may, Tuscans are connoisseurs of the humble bean, and were recognized as such as early as the eighteenth century by the great Neapolitan chef and cookery writer, Vincenzo Corrado. In his celebrated work *Il Cuoco Galante* ("The Gallant Chef"), he claims that, "Florentines, more than all others, know how tasty beans – particularly dried white beans – can be and make great use of them." Since the sixteenth century, when white beans arrived in Europe from the New World, Tuscans have developed several of their own varieties of this favourite food. *Cannellino* – a medium-sized white bean which has now become the most popular bean nationwide – was originally from Tuscany, where the regional variety is called *toscanello.*

A local Tuscan bean, the *zolfino,* a relative of the *toscanello* and indigenous to the province of Arezzo, was formerly on the verge of extinction, but is currently enjoying a revival. The origin of its name, derived from the Italian word for sulphur, *zolfo*, is disputed: some say it is from its pale yellow colour; others claim it is because it was discovered in the Apennine foothills of Arezzo, in the area beneath the Pratomagno mountain range, where there were once sulphuric springs.

The *zolfino*'s precarious state of survival results from the specific agricultural conditions required for its successful cultivation. As its roots need perfect drainage and will not tolerate even a minimum of stagnant water, it cannot be grown on flat land. It also requires soil with a low calcium content and a specific concentration of minerals. Inevitably, in an age of industrial farming, the future of the *zolfino* was in jeopardy. Thanks to the efforts of the "Slow Food Movement" – comprised of producers, retailers, professional promoters and dedicated consumers – the *zolfino* has been saved, and with it a small but important part of Tuscan gastronomy.

The defining botanical characteristic of the *zolfino* is its thin skin, which gives it certain culinary and gastronomic advantages. It does not need to be soaked in water overnight before cooking and, once prepared, its creamy texture melts in your mouth. It is also exceptionally rich in minerals and fibre. Additionally, because of its thin skin, it is more easily digested than other beans and there is less risk of producing embarrassing noises after enjoying a dish or two.

The most celebrated and picturesque way to cook white beans in Tuscany, a method more part of its culinary past than present practice, was *al fiasco* (meaning "wine flask"). Tuscan women put their freshly shelled white beans in an old Chianti flask, the kind that were once popular as candle holders in Italian restaurants, but in this case with the straw removed. They filled the flask with water, added a sage leaf and a garlic clove, placed it in the embers of the hearth where the home fires were kept burning all day, and left it to simmer leisurely away.

Continued on page 85 ☞

SCOTTIGLIA

Mixed braised meats

This dish is typical of the Arezzo culinary tradition. Not only does the province have the best beef in Tuscany, it also has plentiful game and still supports a system of small farming where animals are raised for their meat. Whatever meats are available can go into this delicious stew.

1 kilo/2lb mixed meat (such as chicken, rabbit, pork, veal, hare, lamb, guinea fowl)
1 small carrot, finely chopped
1 celery stalk, finely chopped
1 garlic clove, finely chopped
1 small onion, finely chopped
1 handful flat-leaf parsley, finely chopped
1 bay leaf
90ml/3fl oz/$^{1}/_{3}$ cup extra virgin olive oil
120ml/4fl oz/$^{1}/_{2}$ cup good quality red Chianti wine
480g/17oz fresh plum (peeled not seeded) or canned tomatoes, finely chopped
240ml/8fl oz/1 cup light chicken or veal stock
12 thin slices of coarse country bread, lightly toasted
salt and pepper

1. Divide the meat into pieces, retaining any bones.
2. Fry the carrot, celery, garlic, onion, parsley and bay leaf in the oil on a low heat for about 2 minutes.
3. Raise the heat slightly, add the meat and fry for about 5 minutes, until golden, stirring a couple of times. Add the wine. Stir and cook until evaporated.
4. Add the tomatoes, salt and pepper to taste, cover and cook on a low heat for about 1 hour, or until very tender. Add the stock a little at a time, when necessary, to ensure that the meat remains well moistened.
5. Arrange the bread on a platter, cover with the meats and the juice and allow to stand for a few minutes before serving.

Serves 6

FAGIOLI ALL'UCCELLETTO

Beans in tomato sauce

The literal translation of this dish is "white beans cooked like tiny birds" – a traditional way to cook small game birds in Tuscany is to braise them in a light tomato sauce seasoned with garlic and sage. These beans are often served with pork sausages.

300g/11oz/1 1/2 cups dry white beans, such as *zolfini* or *cannellini*
3 garlic cloves, peeled
1 handful fresh sage leaves
90ml/3fl oz/1/3 cup extra virgin olive oil
300g/11oz fresh plum (peeled not seeded) or canned tomatoes, chopped
salt and pepper

1. Cover the beans with water, slowly bring to the boil and cook covered for about 1 1/2 hours, or until tender. Drain and reserve.
2. Fry the garlic and sage leaves in the oil on a low heat for about 2 minutes, or until barely golden. Add the beans and cover with the tomatoes. Add salt and pepper and cook, stirring occasionally, for about 10 minutes. Ensure that the cooking juices do not dry out.
3. Arrange on a platter and serve.

Serves 6

This method, it is claimed, preserved more of the beans' unique aroma and flavour than is possible in a modern metal pot. Today, it is possible to buy flasks designed specially for cooking beans in this way, but using a very low flame instead. Romola, our family cook at Coltibuono for decades, told me that her mother would leave a terracotta pot of beans covered with water over the dying fire in their wood-burning stove before going to bed. When she removed them from the fire the next morning they would be beautifully cooked. The one essential technique behind these various methods is always to ensure that the beans cook slowly, otherwise they will split open.

Tuscans use white beans as the base for soups such as *minestrone* and *ribollita* (see page 25) and in delicious salads, combined with tuna that has been preserved in extra virgin olive oil, and chopped red onions. As a main dish, they pair them with their tasty pork sausages and simmer them in tomato pulp and extra virgin olive oil, seasoned with fresh rosemary and sage. As mentioned above, white beans are the essential accompaniment to steak as well as to *arista*, Tuscan pork roast. As a side-dish, they are either served simply, seasoned with extra virgin olive oil and lots of black pepper, often at room temperature, or cooked with tomato sauce, *all'uccelletto* (see page 83).

OPPOSITE: The magnificent landscape of Vallombrosa in Arezzo's central Apennines, which so inspired the 17th-century English poet John Milton that he dedicated a passage of his epic poem, Paradise Lost*, to their beauty. ABOVE: Fresh* porcini.

CASTAGNACCIO

Chestnut cake

Two areas in Tuscany are celebrated nationwide for their chestnuts – Casentino in Arezzo and Garfagnana in Lucca (see pages 117–127). This cake is typical of both regions, and is made throughout Tuscany during the chestnut season in mid-autumn. The recipe presented here is very traditional and relies on aromatic rosemary and pinenuts alone to give the unique flavour.

300g/11oz/2 cups chestnut flour
90ml/3fl oz/⅓ cup extra virgin olive oil
360ml/12fl oz/1½ cups water
2 tablespoons fresh rosemary leaves
60g/2oz pinenuts
pinch of salt

1. Preheat the oven to 170°C/325°F.
2. Pour the flour into a bowl, add 2 tablespoons of the oil and the water, a little at a time, mixing carefully to avoid lumps. Add salt.
3. Pour the rest of the oil into a non-stick square or rectangular mould, about 30cm/12in across, and add the batter so that it is approximately 1.5cm/½in thick.
4. Sprinkle the top with the rosemary and the pinenuts and cook in the oven for about 20 minutes, or until the surface begins to crack. Remove from the oven and, with the help of a knife, cut into squares and arrange on a platter. Serve lukewarm or at room temperature.

Serves 6

GROSSETO

AND ITS PROVINCE

In the princely palaces of Rome, Renaissance chefs would often prepare wild boar cooked in a sweet and sour sauce for their patrons' festive banquets. The boar were hunted in Grosseto – the southernmost province of Tuscany. Wild boar still thrive in the lowland wilderness of this region, providing chase for hunters as well as a favourite dish for the Tuscan table.

On the slopes of Grosseto's Monte Amiata, pine forests and chestnut woods create ideal conditions for another kind of hunting. Here, *porcini*, *ovoli* and other varieties of wild mushrooms flourish, offering sport and sustenance for thousands of mushroom gatherers from all over Tuscany. They are prepared baked, grilled and sautéed, and are used in soups and sauces or eaten raw in salads.

When Colonel William "Buffalo Bill" Cody, the legendary character from America's Wild West, was on tour in 1905 with his famous rodeo, he was challenged to a competition with the *butteri* – cowboys from Grosseto's Maremma region. It is said, at least around these parts, that they beat Buffalo Bill's cowboys hands-down. For centuries, the *butteri* have been tending cattle and roaming the Maremma range on their sturdy, locally bred horses. They have become symbolic of the wilderness that characterizes this provincial pocket of southernmost Tuscany.

The Maremma, or seaside marshland, dominates Grosseto's terrain. A vast, flat plain, which rises from below sea-level along the Mediterranean's Tyrrhenian coast to the rolling countryside bordering the province of Siena, the Maremma was originally the territory of the Etruscans, who occupied central Italy before the Roman conquest. They built an efficient canal system to drain the plains, but these were subsequently neglected, and by medieval times had become a breeding ground for malarial mosquitoes. In the nineteenth century, the Austrian Grand Dukes of Tuscany began to reclaim the land, a task completed only under Mussolini's government. It was not until the American army introduced the insecticide known as DDT to the area during the Second World War that the mosquitoes were exterminated.

By late spring, Tuscan fields turn into a grand bouquet of wild flowers – a fragrant mixture of red poppies, purple clover, white Queen Anne's lace, deep-blue cornflowers and pink prime roses.

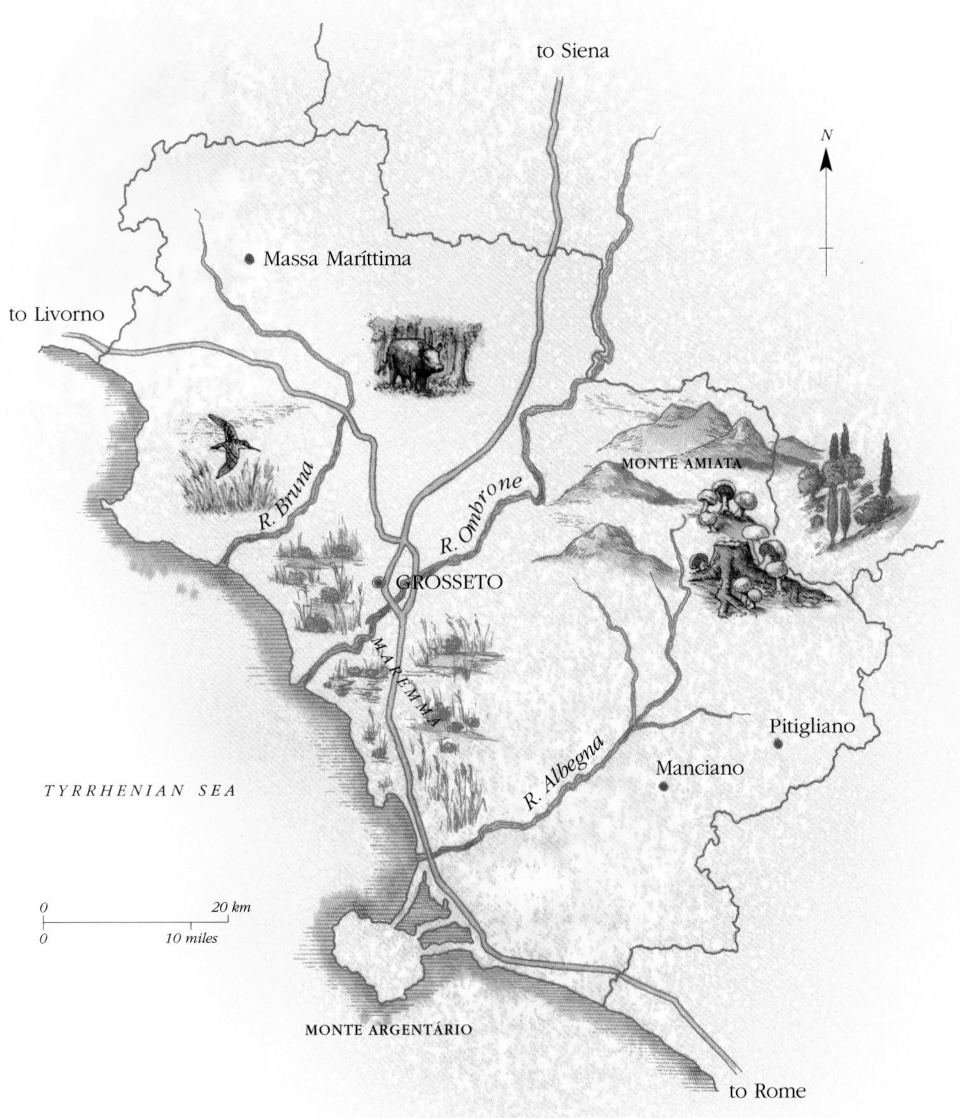
to Siena
N
Massa Maríttima
to Livorno
MONTE AMIATA
R. Bruna
R. Ombrone
GROSSETO
MAREMMA
Pitigliano
Manciano
R. Albegna
TYRRHENIAN SEA
0
20 km
0
10 miles
MONTE ARGENTÁRIO
to Rome

Today, besides the *butteri* and their herds, the Maremma is mainly the domain of Tuscany's plentiful and varied flora and fauna. Much of the area bordering the coastline has been declared a nature reserve, favoured by migratory and many other types of birds, including kingfishers, herons, ducks, hoopoes and falcons. It has now become southern Europe's most popular stop-over for wild geese – more than 700 were counted recently. The terrain is covered in Mediterranean scrub (*macchia*), rosemary, heather, juniper and thickets of arbutus and broom. The almost impenetrable low bush forms an ideal habitat for pheasant, quail, partridges, foxes, weasels, badgers, porcupines, hare, deer and wild boar. During hunting season, the human population of the Maremma is supplemented by hunters and, on Sundays, by diners visiting the restaurants that feature local game on their menus.

Thanks to conservation efforts, deer and other animals are making a gradual comeback in the Tuscan countryside, although wild boar are the only "big game" still plentiful. Prolific as a breed, they constitute a major menace to crops in many areas, especially to Tuscany's grape harvest. In late summer, they come out of hiding after dark to feast on the grapes. Driving at night along country roads, you often catch them in your headlights on their way from one vineyard feast to the next. To control their numbers, local wildlife authorities often give permission for out-of-season shoots. Wild boar, *cinghiali*, are the ancestors of the domestic pig and should not be confused with domestic pigs that have subsequently gone wild, which are also hunted in many parts of the world. In the province of Siena, where the *cinte senesi* (the local breed of pig) are raised free range, they often mate with their wild cousins. Genuine wild boar are becoming increasingly rare worldwide. In some places, they have been hunted to extinction and almost everywhere their natural habitat is diminishing. As a result, they are frequently raised wild

CROSTINI DI FEGATINI

Chicken-liver toast

These tasty crostini *are the most typical of all Tuscan* antipasti. *I have "awarded" them to the province of Grosseto, because in my experience it is where they are most often served warm, which is the most satisfying way to eat them.*

- 1 small onion, finely chopped
- 2 tablespoons extra virgin olive oil
- 60g/2oz unsalted butter
- 6 chicken livers, cleaned
- 2 anchovy fillets preserved in oil, drained and chopped
- 1 tablespoon salted capers, well-washed and chopped
- 60ml/2fl oz/¼ cup dry white wine
- 1 tablespoon brandy
- 3 tablespoons chicken stock
- 18 thin slices coarse country bread, lightly toasted

1. Cook the onion, with the oil and half the butter, on a low heat in a saucepan for about 3 minutes, or until translucent.
2. Add the chicken livers, anchovy fillets and capers, and sauté on a medium heat, stirring often, for about 5 minutes, or until barely golden. Add the wine and the brandy and allow to evaporate.
3. Add the stock and cook for a couple of minutes more. Allow to cool.
4. Take out the chicken livers and chop them finely. Return them to the saucepan with the rest of the butter and reheat for a couple of minutes. Spread on the toast while still warm and serve immediately.

Serves 6

A hunter with his two highly trained wild-boar dogs. Once the dogs have caught the scent of the wild boar and rousted it out of its cover, the hunter has a brief window of opportunity in which to capture his fleeing prey.

in large fenced-off areas of the countryside. In the Maremma they thrive.

Adult boar are huge beasts, black and bristly, weighing 100 kilos (220lb) or more, with impressive tusks. Their appearance is more ferocious than their personality: they are shy and not aggressive, unless cornered or provoked, as hunting dogs inevitably discover. Baby boar, up to the age of six months, are reddish in colour and their fur is striped with dark bands from head to tail. They are not considered fair game until they are three months old. By the time they are two, they will have turned black and their flesh is considered perfect for cooking. After six years or so, they are still edible but their meat is tough and gamey. If they succeed in avoiding the hunters, they can live to a ripe old age. An ancient "hermit" boar, estimated to have been about 30 years old, survived in the woods and forests surrounding Badia a Coltibuono, our family estate, until he finally dropped dead of old age.

Wild boar tend to move around in packs, as do the hunters and their dogs. The humans usually number between 30 and 60, the canines about 20; the wild boar are often in their dozens. Usually, members of the hunting team will encircle an area, forming an armed guard along a valley corridor through which the wild boar is forced to run. At the same time, others stalk the prey with their dogs, who bark in an attempt to chase them from under the thick cover. The territory is wide and the prey extremely wily. They must be shot on the run. An average hunt will usually bring down two or three boar. Traditionally, the innards and the head (the latter is a trophy to be mounted on the wall), go to the hunter who hit the moving target. The rest is divided among the team and taken home to freeze.

In the Maremma, the prized fresh boar innards go into a dish called *corata di cinghiale alla maremmana*. The heart, liver, spleen and lungs (but not the kidneys, which require time-consuming preparation before cooking) are roughly chopped and browned in olive oil and onion, seasoned with wild calamint (*nepitella*) and chilli (called *zenzero* in Tuscany), and then cooked for about ten minutes with chopped mature tomatoes and a little red wine. The hunters often prepare this dish in the woods over an open fire.

Wild boar is prepared in the same ways as its domestic cousin. If it is young and the meat is not tough and gamey, you can grill the ribs and chops, and bake the ham. For more mature animals, the classic preparation, well-known since medieval times, is *cinghiale in agrodolce* (see page 100). The areas in Tuscany that are home to wild boar pride themselves on their processed products of wild boar sausages and *prosciutto*, which are darker in colour and more pronounced in flavour than domestic pork products.

Italy, it is said, has three national sports: soccer, hunting and mushroom gathering. In Tuscany, the first two are currently going through hard times, but the passion for mushrooms flourishes. After the first autumn rains, in late September and October, parked cars line the sides of country roads. Their owners, having abandoned work, household and family for the day, are in the woods hunting for *funghi*, or mushrooms.

Every Tuscan province has a wild mushroom harvest. However, the most abundant harvest is found in the

Continued on page 102 ☞

FOLLOWING PAGE: A fortified farmhouse in the Maremma. For centuries this wild area was a "no man's land" – an ideal hide-out for bandits. The few intrepid landowners living here built these impregnable structures to protect their families.

ACQUACOTTA MAREMMANA

Vegetable egg soup

Acquacotta *means "cooked water", which gives no indication of the deliciousness of this soup, popular in several Tuscan provinces. Grosseto's* Maremmana *version is more hearty than the rest, probably because it is the traditional fare of the local cowboys, the* butteri *(see page 90).*

1 handful sage leaves
60ml/2fl oz/¹/₄ cup extra virgin olive oil
2 handfuls fresh broad (fava) beans, shelled
2 handfuls fresh peas, shelled
1 artichoke, trimmed and finely sliced
1 carrot, peeled and diced
1 celery stalk, trimmed and diced
1 onion, peeled and finely sliced
2 litres/4 pints/8 cups water
1 tablespoon fresh thyme leaves
6 slices coarse bread, lightly toasted
2 garlic cloves, crushed
6 eggs
salt and pepper

1. Cover the bottom of a pot with the sage and the oil. Fry gently on a low heat for about 2 minutes.
2. Add the remainder of the vegetables, stir gently and pour in the water. Bring to the boil and simmer for about 30 minutes. Then sprinkle with the thyme, and add salt and pepper to taste.
3. Brush the bread slices with the garlic and arrange into 6 individual soup bowls. Break an egg into each one and pour the boiling soup on top. Wait a couple of minutes to set the whites, then serve immediately.

Serves 6

CINGHIALE IN AGRODOLCE

Wild boar in sweet and sour sauce

Based on a classic medieval recipe, this is an ideal way to serve the tougher meat of more mature wild boar. Before cooking, the meat is first tenderized by marinading it in a sweet and sour sauce traditionally made with chocolate or sugar and vinegar, and seasoned with herbs.

1 carrot, chopped
1 celery stalk, chopped
1 small onion, chopped
1 handful flat-leaf parsley
1 teaspoon black peppercorns
3 bay leaves, 3 cloves
½ bottle good quality red wine
2 glasses red wine vinegar
2 kilos/4lb wild boar on the bone
60g/2oz *pancetta*, diced
30g/1oz unsalted butter
2 tablespoons plain flour
3 tablespoons granulated sugar
2 garlic cloves, chopped
30g/1oz sultanas soaked in water
30g/1oz pinenuts
60g/2oz candied orange peel, diced
60g/2oz cherries preserved in alcohol
30g/1oz prunes, diced

1. Combine the carrot, celery, onion, parsley, peppercorns, bay leaves, cloves, wine and half the vinegar in a bowl to form a marinade. Place the piece of wild boar in the marinade and let it stand for a couple of days, turning the meat occasionally, until tenderized.
2. Fry the *pancetta* on a low heat until golden for about 5 minutes. Drain the wild boar and add it to the *pancetta*. Cook on medium heat for about 10 minutes, stirring occasionally. Add salt to taste and half the marinade. Cover with a pan lid and simmer gently for about 3 hours, adding the rest of the marinade gradually to keep the mixture moist.
3. Combine the butter and the flour together in a food processor. Drain off the cooking juices from the meat and add to the butter and flour, puréeing the mixture to form a sauce.
4. Place the sauce and the meat in a pan and reheat on a very low heat.
5. Gently heat the sugar, the garlic and the rest of the vinegar in a pan until it has reduced by half. Pour this liquid on top of the wild boar, and stir in the sultanas, the orange peel, cherries and prunes. Heat well, arrange on a platter and serve.

Serves 6

TESTE DI FUNGHI IN CARTOCCIO

Mushroom caps cooked in foil

My favourite way to enjoy a porcini *cap is simply to bake it whole. I take a well-formed cap, wrap it in aluminium foil, add a drizzle of extra virgin olive oil and a sprinkling of fresh herbs, and bake it for 15 minutes.*

18 very firm *porcini* mushroom caps
6 garlic cloves, finely chopped
3 tablespoons flat-leaf parsley, finely chopped
3 tablespoons extra virgin olive oil
salt and pepper

1. Preheat the oven to 200°C/400°F.
2. Wipe the mushrooms with a cloth and place each mushroom on a piece of foil in groups of three.
3. Sprinkle them with the garlic, parsley, olive oil and salt and pepper to taste. Close the foil tightly over each group of mushrooms to form six separate parcels and cook them in the oven for about 15 minutes. Open the parcels slightly and serve them immediately, while still piping hot.

Serves 6 (as a side dish)

pine forests and chestnut woods of Grosseto's Monte Amiata, the highest mountain in southern Tuscany. Here, mushrooms have two seasons, a brief and precarious one in spring, when the woodland soil is still humid but beginning to heat up with the year's first warm days; and a longer, more reliable one in autumn, when the hot, dry earth turns damp after the rains return. Locals say the weather must "make the earth boil" to produce mushrooms. Some years, owing to lack of rain or early frost, virtually none are to be found. Farming wisdom also holds that a good year for wine means a bad year for mushrooms, as grapes mature fully when the autumn is hot and dry. Fortunately, the weather gods frequently time conditions in such a way as to provide generous harvests for both.

When this happens, Tuscans and other Italians as far away as Milan – men and women, young and old, country folk and city-dwellers – take to the woods. Yet this is not a social outing. It is a serious search, and every person has his or her own section of the woods in which they have been lucky before – such locations are kept closely guarded secrets. Once they get

*ABOVE: Wild borage (*borragine*) growing on the hillsides of the Maremma. In spring, women collect this herb and use it to season soups and bean dishes. OPPOSITE: The* melegrana *or pomegranate tree, popular in the gardens of southern Tuscany.*

out of their cars and put on their boots, the gatherers set out, separately, with a basket and small knife in hand. The mushrooms they are hoping to find are *porcini*, the *Boletus edulis* or wild cep. In Italian, the word *porcini* means "little pigs" – an apt description, since they are fat and squat in shape, and reddish-brown in colour. Their stalks or stems are thick and their large round caps have a spongy underside.

Wild mushrooms have an intensity of flavour with which their cultivated cousins cannot compete. The aroma and flavour of *porcini* are rich and complex, reminiscent of the earth and woodland in which they grow. Tuscans eat fresh wild *porcini* in soups and salads and in pasta and meat sauces. Both the cap and the stem are used. Tuscans like to season all their *porcini* dishes with

A view across the rolling hills of the Crete Senesi to the wooded slopes of the sleeping volcano Monte Amiata – the highest peak in southern Tuscany (1,738m/5,720ft).

THE ORBETELLO EEL

In the sea off the southernmost boundary of the province of Grosseto lies the former island of Monte Argentário. In the eighteenth century it was joined to the mainland by two sandy strips of land which form the Orbetello lagoon. The waters of the lagoon are brimming with sea bass, bream and grey mullet. Among them slide fat and tasty *anguille*, European eels.

Today, most Orbetello eels are raised in concrete saltwater pools by the lagoon. When they are ready for the table, they are marinaded in brine, dried in the sun and then covered with hot, sweet peppers, boiled in vinegar and smoked briefly over a wood fire. This procedure is thought to be Spanish, dating back to Spain's occupation of the island in the sixteenth century. Locally smoked Orbetello eels, *anguilla fumata*, are fried in olive oil and served as an *antipasto*.

a sprig of *nepitella,* calamint in English, a type of wild mint – more delicate in flavour than the garden variety – which has violet flowers and small leaves.

Another easy and satisfying way to prepare thick and meaty *porcini* caps is to grill them over hot coals for a few minutes on each side, enough to brown, and, before serving, season them with salt, pepper and a drizzle of extra virgin olive oil. This method works only if you use the biggest and best caps – otherwise, they shrivel on the grill and look pathetic on the plate. I use the smaller caps and stems for soups and sauces. Personally, I prefer a perfectly grilled fresh *porcini* cap to a Chianina steak.

One of the culinary treasures of the Tuscan table are dried *porcini* mushrooms. Their woody, earthy aroma and flavour are concentrated in the drying process to an intensity beyond that of fresh mushrooms. The quality of dried and packaged mushrooms varies greatly. Select those that are creamy in colour and meaty in substance and avoid packets that contain dark, shrivelled pieces. They keep indefinitely, and I recommend to my cookery students that they take a bag back home with them in their suitcase – add a few to *risotto,* or to sauces for pasta and meat, to recreate a fragrant taste of Tuscany all year round.

Another edible wild mushroom found in the Tuscan woods, more rare and costly than the *porcini,* is the *Amanita caesarea.* In Italian it is called *ovolo,* or egg-mushroom, as it is shaped and coloured just like an egg. When they first push up out of the ground they are enclosed in an egg-shaped and egg-coloured "*volva*" that later opens to reveal a beautiful yolk-orange cap. *Ovoli* are always eaten raw, so as to savour to the fullest their delicious, subtle, delicate taste. I think the best way to enjoy them is in a salad, sliced paper-thin, mixed with shavings of fresh parmesan and dressed with olive oil and lemon. With a dusting of white truffles on top, you have created the most heavenly salad on earth.

CENCI

Fried pastry

Cenci *are actually strips of egg pasta, fried and sweetened with sugar. In Tuscany, they are traditionally eaten during Lent and, in former times, were enjoyed as a humble and therefore legitimate indulgence, which sweetened the 40 days' fast prior to Easter.*

300g/11oz/2 cups plain flour
1 tablespoon granulated sugar
2 large eggs, beaten slightly
60g/2oz unsalted butter, melted
1 tablespoon Vin Santo
1 tablespoon grated orange zest
flour for dusting
1 litre/2 pints/4 cups oil for deep-frying
pinch of salt

1. Mix the flour and the sugar in a bowl. Add the eggs (a little at a time so as not to form lumps), the butter, Vin Santo, orange zest and salt to form a smooth paste.
2. On a floured table, thin the paste with a rolling pin to about 3mm/1/8in. Cut into rectangles using a roller with fluted edges.
3. Heat the oil to 170°C/325°F and fry the *cenci*, a few at a time, until slightly golden.
4. Drain on absorbent paper and serve while still warm.

Serves 6

MASSA-CARRARA,

LUCCA, PISTOIA, PRATO AND THEIR PROVINCES

These four neighbouring provinces in northern Tuscany comprise a varied landscape of sea, mountains, remote valleys and historic cities and towns. The provinces' local foods express this diversity. In the mountains, not far from the marble quarries of Carrara in the village of Colonnata, slabs of tasty lard, soft and sweet as butter, are made from locally raised pigs. In the valleys of Lucca, a nutty tasting grain called *farro* is grown and used to thicken hearty soups. Chestnut trees grow on the hills of the same area – their nuts harvested and ground into flour to make traditional sweet dishes, or roasted over the fire for a winter treat. The cities of Prato and Pistoia are celebrated for their *biscotti*, traditional confections made from ancient local recipes.

When I was growing up, I spent a few weeks of every summer with my family at Forte dei Marmi, a small, lively and rather elegant seaside resort in the area of Tuscany known as La Versilia, located in the province of Lucca (see pages 117–27), just over the border from the province of Massa-Carrara. These holidays were my first taste of Tuscany. I still remember swimming in the sea and looking up at the spectacular sight of the Apuan Alps, which slope down so that they almost touch the sandy beach. The peaks of these rugged limestone mountains are so translucently white that they appear to be covered in snow – but, in fact, it is the prestigious marble of Carrara which sparkles under the sun, exposed by centuries of excavations begun in Roman times.

A spectacular view of the town of Carrara from the white slopes of the Carrara marble quarries high up in the rugged Apuan Alps.

Michelangelo is the most famous of the thousands of sculptors who have come to these quarries to select stone for their work. Today, Matthew Spender works there and Botero has his studio in the nearby town of Pietrasanta. A few kilometres above the town of Carrara, up a steeply winding road, lies the ancient Roman settlement of Colonnata, a small

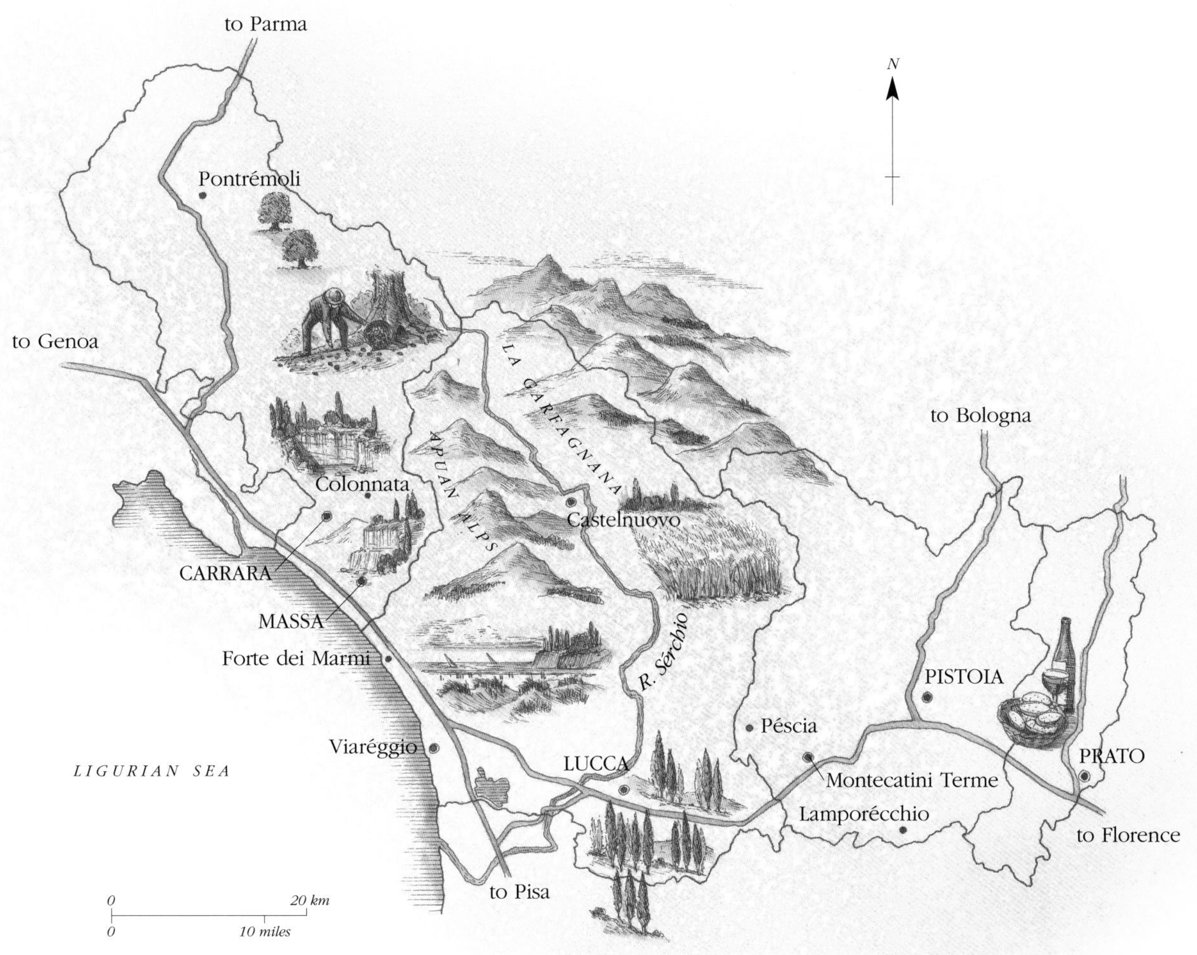
to Parma
N
Pontrémoli
to Genoa
LA GARFAGNANA
to Bologna
APUAN ALPS
Colonnata
Castelnuovo
CARRARA
MASSA
Forte dei Marmi
R. Serchio
PISTOIA
Péscia
Viaréggio
LUCCA
PRATO
LIGURIAN SEA
Montecatini Terme
Lamporécchio
to Florence
0
20 km
0
10 miles
to Pisa

stone village with important marble quarries. Here, a few dedicated artisans produce one of Tuscany's most prized gastronomic specialities, the celebrated *lardo di Colonnata* – Colonnata lard. Curiously, it resembles a small slab of Carrara marble and is aged in tiny troughs carved from the local stone.

For many, the word lard brings to mind chunks of the rancid, yellowish fat, used to moisturize pieces of meat (a process referred to as "larding") in an age when butter and olive oil were not generally available. Colonnata lard is, however, a different food altogether and offers a unique and delicious taste experience.

Lardo di Colonnata is made by extracting the hard layer of fatty connective tissue located directly under the skin of the back of locally raised pigs. This is rendered down within a day after slaughter and cut into slabs weighing around 4 kilos (9lb). These slabs are layered in marble containers, specially made from native stone, which have been rubbed with salt and garlic. The artisan sprinkles each layer with his or her own particular mix of seasonings, which will include pepper, cinnamon, clove, coriander, sage, rosemary and more salt and garlic. The container is then sealed with its marble top and the lard is left to age for a minimum of six months to two years.

Lardo di Colonnata is marble white in colour and streaked with tiny slivers of pink meat. It is eaten in much the same manner as the finest *prosciutto*. In my opinion, it is at its most delicious when prepared as *bruschetta*, cut in ribbon-like slices served on grilled bread (see recipe, opposite). It is also used in cooking to wrap pieces of

Continued on page 117 ☞

FOLLOWING PAGE: One of the many fortified hamlets scattered throughout the Garfagnana – a wild, mountainous part of Lucca, whose forests produce an abundant autumnal harvest of chestnuts and porcini *mushrooms.*

BRUSCHETTA AL LARDO DI COLONNATA

Toasted bread with lard

The gastronomic qualities of lardo di Colonnata *are best enjoyed when it is prepared as* bruschetta*: the heat of the toast melts the lard to a buttery softness and releases the aroma of the seasonings. The taste is exquisite.*

6 slices coarse country bread
6 thin slices Colonnata lard
pepper

1. Toast the bread lightly. When very hot, place the slices of lard on top of the toast - the heat will make them almost transparent.
2. Sprinkle with pepper to taste and serve immediately.

Serves 6

roast meat and game, and to add flavour to bean dishes. In local delicatessens, you will also find *lardone* – lard beaten into a creamy consistency with seasonings added – which is used as a spread. Thanks to vacuum-packing, you can now add a slab of *lardo di Colonnata* to your list of Tuscan culinary treasures to bring back home. You can even buy this product in a miniature marble bowl – a souvenir of two of Tuscany's most prestigious products.

The province of Lucca is perhaps the most varied in all of Tuscany. In just two hours you can drive from the marble quarries around Carrara, along the Versilia coast, and down into the fertile valley surrounding Lucca, with its splendid villas and celebrated gardens. Keep going northeast along the River Sérchio and you enter a wild area, the Garfagnana, situated between Tuscany's two mountain ranges, the Apuan Alps and the Apennines.

This was once the poorest and most isolated region in Tuscany, where the inhabitants survived

OPPOSITE: The Archangel Michael stands at the apex of the ornate façade of the Romanesque church dedicated to him in Lucca's central piazza. ABOVE: A view across the rooftops of Lucca, a charming town barely touched by modern additions.

BUCCELLATO DI LUCCA

Lucca is perhaps the most gracious of all Tuscan cities. At its centre is the Piazza di San Michele, site of the ancient Roman Forum and where today's citizens gather to socialize. Their activities are watched over by a splendid statue of San Michele, the Archangel Michael, atop the lively Romanesque façade of his church.

In the piazza you will find the pastry shop of Mario Taddeucci with its art nouveau front and windows displaying Lucca's gastronomic speciality, *buccellato* - a sweet, ring-shaped bread made with flour, milk, butter, eggs and sugar, studded with raisins and flavoured with aniseed. Like many rich and festive breads, *buccellati* originally had a religious significance and was the traditional gift of godparents to their godchild on the occasion of his or her Confirmation. Today, *buccellati* are baked and enjoyed all year round.

mostly on two local products: *farro* and chestnuts. Ironically, *farro*, emmer in English, has recently become quite fashionable and is now featured on the menus of refined European and New World restaurants.

Brought to Italy by the Greeks centuries before the Christian era, *farro* is the oldest cultivated cereal used in cooking. It was introduced into the Garfagnana by the Roman legions, who ate it as energy food for their long marches and bloody battles – it thrived in the area's poor soil and high altitude. It is still cultivated on a small scale today, and, owing to its recent popularity, other farms outside the Garfagnana have begun producing it. *Farro della Garfagnana* is protected by a consortium whose members use organic farming methods.

Farro kernels are relatively long, oval in shape and are split into two parts on one side. They are golden brown in colour and when the outer skin is polished, parts of the grain show their off-white interior. It is difficult to describe the flavour of *farro*: it is

MINESTRA DI FARRO

Emmer soup

Emmer is put to all the same uses as wheat, including making bread, pasta and even pastry. It can also be boiled like rice and dressed as a salad. But the most traditional and satisfying way to enjoy it is as described here, mixed with vegetables in a hearty soup.

300g/11oz/2 cups emmer

2 litres/4 pints/8 cups water

1 small onion, finely chopped

60ml/2fl oz/1/4 cup extra virgin olive oil

1 carrot, diced

1 small zucchini, diced

1 celery stalk, diced

1 handful peas, shelled

salt and pepper

1. Cover the emmer with water and soak for about 12 hours. Drain the emmer, discarding the water.
2. Fry the onion in the oil for about 3 minutes on a low heat, until translucent.
3. Add the carrot, zucchini, celery, peas and emmer. Mix and cover with 2 litres of water. Bring to a gentle boil and cook for about 1 hour on a low heat.
4. Sprinkle with salt and pepper, pour into a soup tureen and serve immediately.

Serves 6

slightly sweet and nutty and tastes a little like barley – it reminds me of the crust of good country bread.

Until after the Second World War, the other staple food of the Garfagnana's peasants was chestnuts. They are highly nutritious and energy rich, containing potassium and vitamins B and C. They also have a high starch content and much less oil than other nuts, and are therefore suitable for grinding into flour to make bread and other foods. Historians credit the chestnut for having saved generations of Tuscany's remote mountain communities from starvation.

In late autumn, the chestnut and mushroom seasons overlap, keeping intrepid foragers (both professional and amateur) exceptionally busy supplying these two seasonal ingredients to Tuscan cooks to make delicious local dishes.

CHESTNUT-BLOSSOM HONEY

Before the chestnut tree produces its ample autumn harvest of red-brown nuts, it provides another delicious food. In late spring, the tree blossoms in tiny flowers that bud within greenish-yellow cases called catkins. The flowers attract a species of local bee named the *ligustica*, which are found in the hills and mountains of Tuscany. They are endowed with exceptionally long tongues, which enable them more easily to collect nectar from the hard-to-reach chestnut blossoms. The bees then transform this nectar into a delicious honey.

Chestnut-blossom honey has a deep amber colour, pungent aroma and a rich nutty flavour with a pleasingly bitter aftertaste. One of my family's favourite ways to enjoy it is as an ice-cream topping. Simply heat the honey in a small saucepan and, while it is still hot, drizzle it over rich vanilla ice cream.

SEPPIE IN ZIMINO

Cuttlefish with spinach

This is the classic way to prepare cuttlefish along the north Tuscan coast. Cuttlefish are related to squid and octopus, but are smaller, more tender and harder to clean because their bodies contain a small shell or "bone". Chopped beet greens are sometimes used in this recipe instead of spinach.

3 garlic cloves, finely chopped
60ml/2fl oz/¼ cup extra virgin olive oil
1 pinch dried chilli
600g/20oz cuttlefish, cleaned and roughly cut
1 kilo/2lb fresh spinach
300g/11oz fresh plum tomatoes (peeled not seeded), chopped
pinch of salt

1. Fry the garlic in the oil gently for about 2 minutes. Add the chilli and the cuttlefish and sauté on a medium heat until the cuttlefish become red (about 5 minutes).
2. Add the spinach, the tomatoes and salt to taste. Lower the heat, cover and cook for 10 minutes more. If there appears to be too much liquid, allow to evaporate without the lid.
3. Arrange on a platter and serve.

Serves 6

CARCIOFI AL FUNGHETTO

Sautéed artichokes

Al funghetto *is a term used in northern Italy and Liguria to describe a method of cooking that elsewhere is called* trifolato, *or "truffled".* Funghi *are often cooked in this way (hence the name), but sliced vegetables, such as eggplant and zucchini, can be prepared in the same manner.*

6 artichokes
bowl of water
juice of 1 lemon
2 garlic cloves, chopped
90ml/3fl oz/$^1/_3$ cup extra virgin olive oil
1 tablespoon flat-leaf parsley, finely chopped
salt and pepper

1. Trim the artichokes, discarding the hard outer leaves and furry choke and cut each one vertically into 4 parts. Arrange them immediately in a bowl filled with the water and lemon juice to prevent discoloration. Drain and pat dry.
2. Fry the garlic in the oil for a couple of minutes, until barely golden. Add the artichokes and cover the pan. Cook for about 10 minutes on a low heat, stirring occasionally. Uncover, add salt and pepper to taste, sprinkle with the parsley, mix well and serve.

Serves 6

through the winter months – they were named *secchielli* ("lovely little dried [nuts]").

Centuries before Columbus brought maize back from the New World, *polenta*, now made with cornmeal, was originally made from chestnuts. In the Garfagnana area, you can still buy *polentine dolci*, "sweet polenta slices". Chestnut flour, referred to as *farina dolce*, "sweet flour", is used for many local dishes. *Necci* – flat cakes – are perhaps the most traditional and ancient. They are baked on hot stones or over the fire between two metal discs with a long handle called *testi*. There is a Tuscan saying that defines the people from the Garfagnana as "those who live where bread finishes and *necci* begin". Nowadays, *necci* are prepared for festivals and markets and are eaten like crêpes, filled with fresh *ricotta*.

The most widely known Tuscan dish made with chestnut flour is undoubtedly *castagnaccio* (see page 87). It is a curious semi-sweet flat cake, traditionally baked in a large, round copper pan. Into the chestnut batter goes a selection from pine nuts, raisins, fennel seeds and often rosemary. According to traditional recipes it should be cooked until it is brown and cracked, with the appearance of "parched earth". On the inside it should be pinkish in colour and have a deliciously soft, moist consistency.

As you drive from Lucca to Florence, you pass along a valley road, flanked on the north by the Apennines, through two Tuscan provinces, Pistoia and Prato. Both

Prato's medieval cathedral, whose façade is partially composed of alternating blocks of green and white stone. On one corner of the building is its celebrated outdoor pulpit, with a fan-shaped canopy, designed by Michelozzo in the 15th century.

The lengthy process for making Vin Santo, Tuscany's famous dessert wine, begins with a careful selection of Malvasia and Trebbiano grapes from the vine. The bunches are dried for several weeks by hanging them from rafters or spreading them out on mats. Then they are crushed and the juice is put in barrels, which are placed in lofts to ferment for several years.

VIN SANTO

Vin Santo, or "holy wine", is considered Tuscany's most precious wine. It is produced in limited quantities by a long and painstaking process, using the finest white grapes. The result is a golden- or amber-coloured wine, which comes in varying degrees of sweetness and possesses a complex aroma and taste. The finest Vin Santo has rich flavours of vanilla, honey and almonds. It is often served with *biscotti di Prato* (see recipe, page 131), which are dipped into it. When I serve our excellent Vin Santo di Coltibuono, I encourage my guests to first savour the wine on its own before dipping.

There have been various explanations of how Vin Santo acquired its name. Probably the most plausible is that it was, and still is, considered the wine most worthy to be used in the celebration of the Holy Eucharist, the Catholic liturgy of the Mass.

are surrounded by sprawling industrial areas and large suburbs, yet they possess ancient and splendid historic centres enclosed within medieval walls, which contain masterpieces of art and architecture.

Pistoia, Tuscany's smallest province, known since medieval times for its metalworks, is now important for its significant involvement in railway construction. Within the province, the town of Péscia, situated in a fertile plain, is home to one of the most prominent plant nurseries in Italy, and exports Italian varieties of olive tree as far as New Zealand and California. Also located in Pistoia is the famous international spa, Montecatini Terme. The city of Prato, the third largest Tuscan city after Florence and Livorno, has been one of Europe's major textile-manufacturing cities since the thirteenth century. A chapel in its ancient cathedral is not only decorated with sculptures and paintings by renowned medieval and Renaissance artists, but also houses a venerated relic – the Virgin's girdle.

With regard to fine food, both Pistoia and Prato are famous for their confectionery – a traditional speciality of rich merchant cities, as only the wealthy could afford the then rare ingredients necessary for their production. Perhaps the best known of these local confections are *biscotti di Prato* (see recipe, opposite), almond biscuits from Prato, imitations of which are produced throughout Tuscany, Italy and even the United States. They were put on the gastronomic map in 1858, when Antonio Mattei opened a small bakery in the city and began producing these biscuits according to an ancient tradition. They are popularly known as *cantucci* as they are crunchy and "sing" (*cantare*) when bitten into. The Antico Biscottificio Antonio Mattei is still baking these traditional cookies under the direction of three generations of the Pandolfini family in the original establishment on Via Ricasoli in the historic centre of Prato.

Since medieval times, cloistered nuns often made special confections as a way of supporting themselves. They had the necessary time and dedication, and the expensive ingredients required were donated to them as a kind of culinary alms. Centuries ago, the Brigidine nuns of the Convent of Saint Brigit in the town of Lamporécchio outside of Pistoia originated a unique sweet subsequently named *brigidini*, after them.

Brigidini are golden-brown, crunchy, curvy wafers, as thin and light as Holy Communion hosts. They are made from a batter of flour, sugar or honey and eggs, flavoured with aniseed. Originally, they were produced with a special implement called a *tenaglia*, a kind of waffle-iron in scissor form with two metal discs, which were often engraved with decorative religious symbols. The iron was left on the fire for only a very few minutes. Today, *brigidini* are made industrially with special machines and by artisan bakers at open-air festivals and markets. They are a favourite family sweet for children as well as adults. I like to serve them with ice cream or cooked fruit desserts.

BISCOTTI DI PRATO

Almond biscuits from Prato

Traditionally these delicious biscuits are baked twice and it is this process that gives them their characteristic texture – crunchy but not hard. This is a simpler version of the recipe. The biscuits keep well in a tin and soften deliciously when dipped into a glass of Vin Santo, Tuscan sweet wine.

300g/11oz/2½ cups plain flour
2 teaspoons baking powder
150g/5oz/⅔ cup granulated sugar
2 whole eggs plus 2 egg yolks
120g/4oz almonds, chopped
1 tablespoon milk

1. Preheat the oven to 180°C/350°F.
2. In a bowl, mix the flour with the baking powder, sugar, 2 whole eggs, 1 of the egg yolks and the almonds, and work until a soft dough is formed. Divide the dough into long sausages, about 2cm/1in thick, and cut into pieces of approximately 3cm/1½in long.
3. Line a baking sheet with greaseproof paper and arrange the biscuits on it. Cook them in the oven for about 20 minutes. Take them out of the oven and allow to cool.
4. Beat the remaining yolk with the milk and brush over the biscuits. Finish them in the oven for 10 minutes more, or until golden. Allow them to cool before serving.

Serves 6

LIVORNO,

PISA AND THEIR PROVINCES

You never feel far from the sea in Tuscany, with its hundreds of kilometres of glorious coastline. Markets in the region's major cities offer an abundant supply of fresh fish and, over the centuries, ports such as Livorno have created mouthwatering fish dishes, including *cacciucco*, a thick fish stew, and *baccalà alla livornese*, salt cod in fresh tomato sauce. Blue-fin tuna is fished in the waters off the island of Elba: the succulent, fatty steaks are often simply sautéed fresh – but this is just one of several traditional ways to prepare this delicious seafood. Not far from the sea, buried in the hills of the province of Pisa, lies the white truffle – the most precious treasure of Tuscan gastronomy. This delicacy appears on the table in late autumn and provides the grand finale of the seasonal Tuscan food cycle.

Tuscany is graced with more than 400 kilometres (250 miles) of Mediterranean coastline, as well as one large island, Elba (which was Napoleon's home in exile), and a number of smaller islands. In medieval times, the Independent Republic of Pisa was the dominant political, military and economic maritime power, not only of Tuscany but (along with Genoa and Venice) of the entire Mediterranean region. At the peak of its prosperity, Pisa controlled trade as far away as Syria. However, in the fifteenth century, everything except its teetering tower seemed to collapse. The harbour at the mouth of the Arno River silted up, meaning that Pisa, 10 kilometres (6 miles) from the coast, could no longer function as a thriving port. Then the powerful Medici family took over the area, leaving Pisa subject to the rule of Florence, and no longer a powerful state in its own right. Today, the largest commercial harbour in Tuscany is situated in neighbouring Livorno, which produces some of the region's finest and most varied seafood.

Tuscany's most famous fish dish, *cacciucco* (a rich, thick, almost stew-like, soup), has its origins in

Continued on page 139 ☞

The picturesque harbour of Portoferráio, which nestles amid steep hills on the northern coastline of the island of Elba.

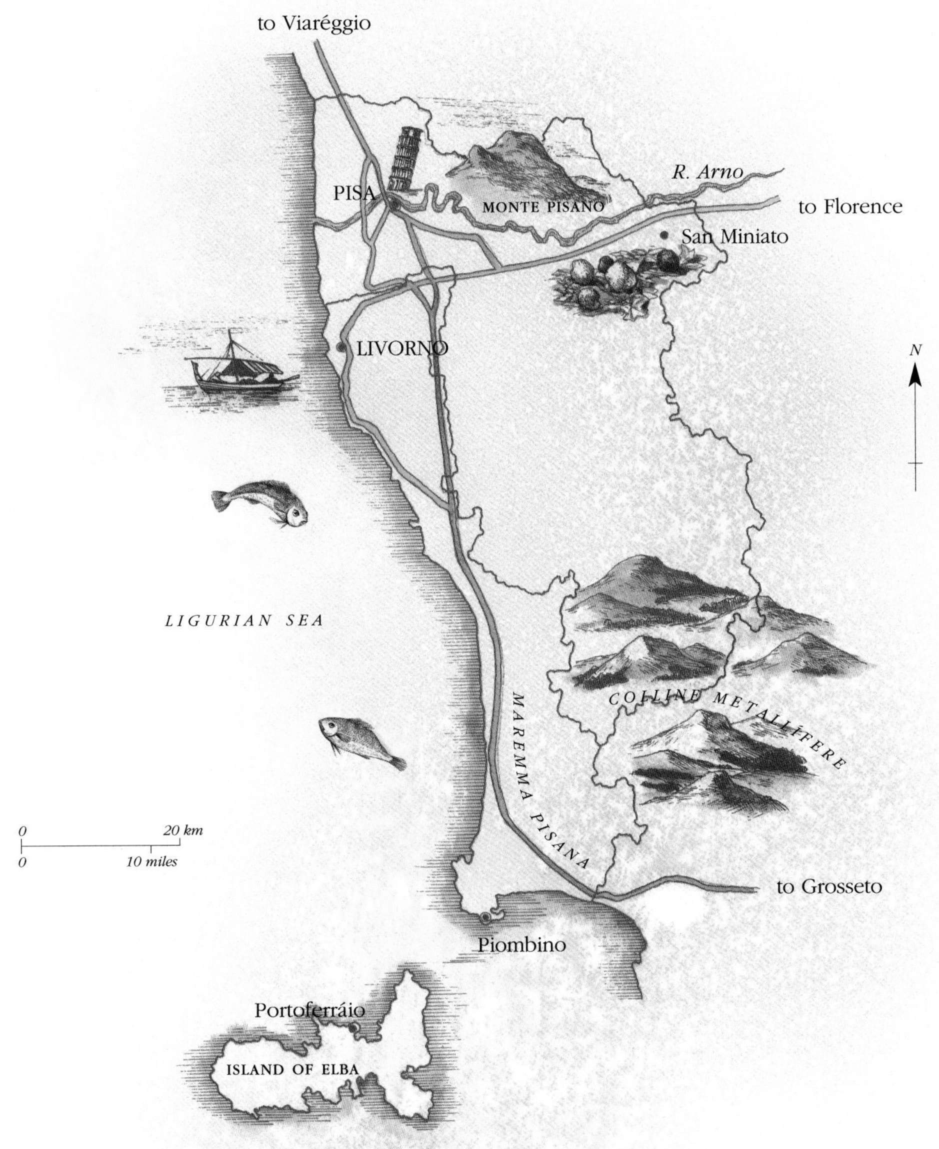

to Viaréggio
PISA
MONTE PISANO
R. Arno
to Florence
San Miniato
LIVORNO
N
LIGURIAN SEA
MAREMMA PISANA
COLLINE METALLIFERE
0
20 km
0
10 miles
to Grosseto
Piombino
Portoferráio
ISLAND OF ELBA

FIORI DI ZUCCA RIPIENI D'ACCIUGHE

Zucchini flowers stuffed with anchovies

Acciughe, *anchovies, are a speciality of the island of Elba, where they are preserved in Tuscan olive oil, rather than salted and canned. Yellow zucchini flowers are a delicacy of late spring and early summer. The decisive flavour of anchovy is a pleasing contrast to the mildness of the zucchini flowers. This is a delicious dish to serve as an appetizer with a glass of chilled white wine.*

300g/11oz zucchini flowers

6 anchovy fillets, stored in oil and drained

120g/4oz/1 cup plain flour

240ml/8fl oz/1 cup sparkling water

1 large egg, well-beaten

1 litre/2 pints/4 cups oil for deep-frying

pinch of salt

1. Clean, but do not wash, the zucchini flowers. Open them slightly and fill with a small piece of anchovy fillet.
2. Make a batter, mixing the flour with the water, a little at a time to prevent lumps; then adding the egg and a pinch of salt.
3. Heat the oil in a frying pan to 170°C/325°F. Dip the flowers in the batter and fry them, a few at a time, in the hot oil until they are golden brown.
4. Drain on absorbent paper and serve immediately, piping hot.

Serves 6

Livorno's vast and lively fish market. Before cleaning up after work, the fishmongers would place a pot over the bonfires that had warmed them during the day and add to it a little olive oil, some parsley and garlic, a tomato or two, and a generous pinch of *zenzero* (the Tuscan word for chilli), which gives this dish its particular zing. Then they would put in their unsold fish and a splash of the local white wine and allow the soup to simmer until they had completed their chores and were ready to eat. Today, *cacciucco* is a popular dish in fish restaurants up and down the Tuscan Tyrrhenian coast (a similar fish soup, *brodetto*, is made along the Adriatic).

The word *cacciucco*, Baltic in origin, means "mixture", and, indeed, there is no set recipe for the particular mixture that constitutes authentic *cacciucco*. Some claim that at least five different fish should be used – one for each "c" in *cacciucco*. Traditionally the soup would include whatever common fish was in season, as well as the "poor" but flavourful fish often left over at market, such as dogfish, catfish and a Mediterranean fish called *scorfano rosso* – red scorpion fish. A few crustaceans, such as shrimps, are essential to the mix, as are cuttlefish, squids and little octopuses. Unscrupulous cooks sometimes cheat and weight the mixture too heavily in favour of an unpopular fish. But the basic principle of the recipe is to keep it true to its origins – cheap and simple (lobster would look and taste incongruous in this dish). Personally I find the pleasure of *cacciucco* is in being presented with a mix of many different kinds of seafood. A rule of my own is, during preparation, to eliminate any

One of the many versions of cacciucco, *Livorno's traditional fish soup, which includes a variety of small, tasty fish, crustaceans and molluscs, stewed in olive oil, tomato, garlic, chilli and a splash of white wine.*

LEGHORN CHICKENS

In Renaissance Italian, the word for Livorno was Legorno, which the British, in their inimitable way, anglicized into "Leghorn" - the term continued to be used by them until well after the Second World War.

In the nineteenth century, Britain began to import a local breed of Mediterranean chicken from Livorno, which they still call the Leghorn White. It has fine-grained white flesh and, producing up to 280 eggs per year, is considered a superior "layer", both in quality and quantity. When this native Livorno chicken arrived in England, it was crossed with an Asiatic breed and was eventually exported to North America, where it evolved into the industrial giant, the Rhode Island Red. Today, descendants of the original free-range Leghorn Whites have been reintroduced to their native Livorno as Rhode Island Reds.

bones – something cooks frequently fail to do. *Cacciucco* is a type of *zuppa*, a thick soup ladled over a slice of grilled country bread.

Another Livorno fish speciality is *baccalà*, or salt-dried cod – perhaps a somewhat surprising product from an area with such an abundance of fresh fish. Cod is not found in Mediterranean waters but is fished in the North Sea surrounding Scandinavia and the northern Atlantic, notably around Newfoundland, and has been imported into southern Europe since medieval times. In Catholic countries – particularly in the inland regions of France, Spain, Portugal and Italy, where fresh fish was rare – dried cod, which could be transported economically, was in great demand. It provided an easy and excellent source of nourishment through periods of religious abstinence from meat.

There are two types of dried cod. Stockfish, *stoccafisso* in Italian, is an entire cod which, traditionally, is air-dried on a stick until it is hard. *Baccalà* is salt cod,

SPAGHETTI ALL'ASTICE

Spaghetti with lobster sauce

As I recall, large lobsters, or astici, *have never been plentiful in the Italian Mediterranean. However, off the coast of Livorno, a related species,* aragosta, *is fished and many consider it to be even more tasty than its cousin. But pasta dressed with any kind of lobster is a delicacy.*

1 lobster, weighing about 1 kilo/2lb
3 garlic cloves, chopped
1 small red chilli, chopped
60ml/2fl oz/¼ cup extra virgin olive oil
300g/11oz fresh plum tomatoes (peeled not seeded), chopped
2 tablespoons flat-leaf parsley, finely chopped
600g/20oz spaghetti
salt

1. Bring a pot of water to the boil, add the lobster and cook for about 10 minutes. Drain (reserving the water) and allow to cool. Peel and then chop the meat roughly.
2. Fry the garlic and chilli in the oil on a low heat for about 2 minutes. Add the lobster and salt to taste, and sauté, stirring for 2 minutes more. Add the tomatoes and the parsley and cook until the liquid has evaporated. Reboil the water in which the lobster was cooked, add salt and the spaghetti. Cook until *al dente*, drain and add the spaghetti to the lobster sauce. Stir on a medium heat for about 2 minutes.
3. Arrange on a platter and serve.

Serves 6

Baccalà alla livornese – *a classic dish in which pieces of salt cod are gently fried in extra virgin olive oil, seasoned with aromatic rosemary and pungent garlic and then simmered in a fresh tomato sauce comprising onion, more garlic, a generous pinch of chilli and a sprinkling of freshly chopped parsley.*

large chunks of cod that are salted on board ship and then partially or lightly dried on land. Although Venetians call the dried cod that is popular in their regional recipes *baccalà*, it is really *stoccafisso* (elsewhere in Italy, *baccalà* always refers to salted, lightly dried cod). Paradoxically, today, when abstinence is rarely observed, *baccalà* has become more popular than ever – it is no longer considered a "penitential fish", but rather a delicacy, the supply of which is scarce.

Baccalà is prepared in many different ways, but the salt must always first be eliminated. Traditionally, it was left under running water for 24 hours but nowadays it is sold already prepared. A friend of mine, the chef and owner of one of America's top restaurants, once confessed to me that the first time they prepared *baccalà*, no one in the kitchen knew that it had to be de-salted. As it was the only main course on that night's menu, all she could do was encourage her guests to drink more wine.

In Livorno, pieces of *baccalà*, deboned but with the skin attached, are lightly floured and fried in extra virgin olive oil with a sprig of rosemary and a garlic clove. Then they are left to simmer for a few minutes in a sauce based on fresh tomatoes, a small onion, several garlic cloves and a pinch of chilli. It is served sprinkled with freshly chopped parsley. *Baccalà alla livornese* is tender and flavourful and when made with high quality salt cod, will break into soft flakes on the fork.

Tuscany has a hoard of buried treasure of inestimable gastronomic value that can be found in several "secret" sites throughout the region. One of the richest deposits lies hidden beneath the earth in the hills and valleys surrounding the small town of San Miniato, not far from Pisa. Toward the end of October, Tuscan treasure hunters and their dogs set out for these parts in search of the *tartufo bianco*, the precious white truffle. Its scientific

Continued on page 146 ☞

ALLA LIVORNESE

So celebrated has Livorno become for the cooking of fish that, throughout Italy, recipes and menu entries often include the term *alla livornese*, "in the style of Livorno". This refers to fish that has been lightly floured, fried in extra virgin olive oil and simmered in a fresh tomato sauce seasoned with a little onion, garlic and chopped parsley.

A light hand is called for throughout this simple cooking process – the less you do to fish, particularly delicate white-fleshed fish, the better. The sauce should retain a fresh tomato taste and should not be too thick or drown the fish.

Salt cod (*baccalà*), red mullet (*triglie*), sole, (*sogliola*) and fresh tuna (*tonno*) are among the main varieties of fish that you will often find prepared *alla livornese*.

ZUPPA DI COZZE

Mussel soup

During the summer, when my family was young, we often sailed off the coast of Tuscany's main islands, Elba and Giglio. In the early morning, we picked mussels clinging to the rocks and in just a few minutes I would prepare this very simple soup for lunch.

3 kilos/6lb mussels
3 fresh plum tomatoes (peeled not seeded), chopped
120ml/4fl oz/½ cup dry white wine
3 tablespoons flat-leaf parsley, finely chopped
3 garlic cloves, whole
6 slices coarse country bread, lightly toasted
salt and pepper

1. Wash and scrub the mussels carefully and place in a large pot. Add the tomatoes, wine, parsley, garlic cloves and salt and pepper to taste. Cover and cook on a medium heat for about 5 minutes or until the mussels open.
2. Arrange the bread in a bowl, pour the mussels and the juice on top and serve immdiately.

Serves 6

PEPERONI AL FORNO

Roasted peppers

I particularly like the combination of this colourful, warm-weather vegetable, and its full, rich taste, with the mussel soup (see opposite). The oregano seasoning brings out perfectly the flavours of both the tomatoes and the mussels.

3 peppers, red
3 peppers, yellow
3 tablespoons extra virgin olive oil
1 tablespoon dried oregano
pinch of salt

1. Preheat the oven to 180°C/350°F.
2. Halve the peppers and discard the seeds. Arrange them on an oiled baking tray and cook them in the oven for about 30 minutes. When cooked, place them in a sealed plastic bag for about 5 minutes. When you remove them from the bag you will be able to peel them more easily.
3. Peel and slice the peppers and arrange them on a platter.
4. Drizzle the oil on top of the peppers, sprinkle with the oregano, add salt to taste and serve them warm or at room temperature.

Serves 6

TUSCAN CHOCOLATES

Italy has been manufacturing fine chocolate since the seventeenth century, especially in the region of Piedmont. Recently, however, a chocolatier in the province of Pisa has begun producing what has been extolled as Italy's best chocolate. Alessio Tessieri, with his sister, Cecilia, are the first chocolate-makers in Italy to import their cacao from Chuao, Venezuela, where the world's premier chocolate beans are grown and dried. They are also the only Italian manufacturers to control the entire complex chocolate-making process, from plantation to finished product.

They produce a limited line of chocolates and pralines; each contains 70 per cent cacao. The flavour is arresting, concentrated, deep and richly satisfying. Their products can be purchased in fine food and wine shops throughout Tuscany.

name is *Tuber magnatum Pico*, "The Great Pico Tuber", named after the eighteenth-century botanist, Signor Pico, who first classified it. White truffles are the most expensive food known to humankind. Depending on the season and the number of links in the supply-chain, they can cost several thousand dollars per kilo.

Truffles are fungi which grow entirely underground, attaching themselves for nourishment to the roots of certain trees. The exact conditions under which they develop remain a mystery but seem to involve a complex relationship between tree, soil and climate (oak, limestone and humidity are common components in ensuring their successful development). The prerequisites for their growth are present in only a few fortunate areas: France's Périgord region is famous for the black truffle, *Tuber melanosporum*, which also grows in Italy (mainly in Umbria but also in Tuscany). Italians consider the black truffle to be a respectable yet poor cousin to the white truffle, whose aroma and taste is

Splendid, perfectly formed specimens of Tuscan white truffles (tartufi bianchi*). Often regarded as the most expensive food known to humankind, white truffles are literally worth their weight in gold. During the truffle season, serious gourmets become gourmands as they shave these precious tubers with expensive abandon over their favourite dishes.*

unique. White truffles command a price many times greater than black truffles.

As they grow wholly underground, finding these precious white truffles is a veritable treasure hunt. A *tartufaio*, a licensed truffle hunter and member of a regional consortium that regulates the activity, can often earn more in a good three-month season than in a year-round job. In the past, hunters used sows to snort out the truffles, but today, specially trained dogs – usually small, short-haired and intelligent cross-breeds – do the job faster and better. It was always difficult to convince a pig to give up its prize, but a dog can be coaxed away with a biscuit, a pat and a modicum of praise.

Truffle-hunting requires considerable skill on the part of both humans and canines. The truffle's aroma can be traced above ground by the dog, but only when the fungus reaches maturity – so, a dog may detect nothing one day, whereas the very next day it may begin to dig at the same spot with great excitement. The *tartufaio* will reward the dog before it actually reaches the truffle, and will continue the digging himself with a *vaghetto*, a small spade with a short wooden handle.

With luck, they will find a firm, tan-coloured nugget (white truffles are "white" only in contrast to black truffles, which resemble pieces of coal). Truffles range in size from that of a hazelnut to that of a small orange. If the soil in which they grow is loose they will be smooth and round; but if they have to struggle for space, they tend to be pitted and gnarled. On the inside they are beige, often finely veined with pinkish streaks.

Two highly trained, obedient and agile truffle-hunting dogs sniff the air for the subtle scent of mature white truffles, which lurk silently beneath the earth.

The aroma (and consequently the taste) of a white truffle is so unusual that it virtually defies description and has become a sensory reference point in itself. The bouquet of certain fine wines, for example, is often described as having the scent of truffles. The fragrance is penetrating, pungent and musky – the aroma of several white truffles in a room can be almost intoxicating.

At the table, white truffles are always eaten raw, and are shaved over food in flakes, as generously as your bank account will allow. Warm food releases the aroma significantly. I find the most satisfying way to enjoy a truffle is to include a lot of it on one dish rather than to use it sparingly on several. The dish itself should be uncomplicated so that it does not distract from the taste of the truffle. Some classic truffle dishes are: *crostini*, little toasts spread with butter and truffles; a salad of truffles and slices of parmesan cheese; *taglierini*, long, thin, home-made noodles tossed in butter and truffles; and *scaloppine*, veal escalopes sautéed in wine and presented with a shaving of truffles. A family favourite is fried eggs, sunny-side-up, with truffle flakes. My personal preference for an elegant, unforgettable supper is a nest of creamy *polenta*, topped with an egg that has been lightly fried in butter. Let your guests shave the truffle themselves.

During the month of November, at the height of white truffle season, the medieval hill town of San Miniato hosts a weekend fair to celebrate its prestigious local food. Truffle enthusiasts from all over Tuscany, *tartufai*, restaurateurs, gourmets and gourmands gather together to sell, buy and, of course, eat white truffles. Competitions among truffle-hunting dogs are held; truffle snacks are sold at stalls; and local restaurants feature extravagant menus based entirely on white truffles. The season also coincides with the release of the region's new harvest wine and freshly pressed extra virgin olive oil. The event is a grand celebration of Tuscany's gastronomic treasures.

TORTA DI MELE E PINOLI

Apple and pinenut cake

The north Tuscan coastline is characterized by stretches of magnificent umbrella pine trees. The nuts from these Mediterranean stone pines are particularly soft and sweet and are incorporated into many outstanding Italian recipes, including the delicious dessert described here.

1 kilo/2lb Golden Delicious apples
2 eggs, large
120g/4oz/1 cup plain flour
120g/4oz/½ cup granulated sugar
120g/4oz unsalted butter, melted
1 teaspoon baking powder
grated zest of 1 lemon
120g/4oz pinenuts

1. Preheat the oven to 180°C/350°F.
2. Peel the apples and slice them finely.
3. In a bowl, mix the eggs, flour, sugar, butter and baking powder to obtain a thick batter. Mix this batter with the apples, the lemon zest and half the pinenuts, and place into a buttered and floured cake pan of about 21cm/8in diameter. Sprinkle the remaining pinenuts on top.
4. Cook in the oven for about 50 minutes, covering the surface with foil after 30 minutes.
5. Release the cake from the pan with the help of a knife and arrange on a serving dish. Allow to cool to room temperature before serving.

Serves 6

DIRECTORY

On these pages I list places where you can be sure to get a genuine and delicious taste of many of the local products featured in the pages of this book. However, these are simply suggestions, intended to get you started on a gastronomic journey through the provinces of Tuscany that could last for literally a lifetime – as it has for me.

SIENA AND ITS PROVINCE

Olio di oliva extra vergine

EXTRA VIRGIN OLIVE OIL

Tuscany is blessed with an abundant supply of high-quality extra virgin olive oil. My favourite, of course, is the oil from our family estate, Badia a Coltibuono. I would recommend two varieties in particular, *Albereto* and *Campo Corto* – both organic, and produced and bottled on our estate. Our olive oils are also exported around the world and can usually be purchased in fine food stores and delicatessens. However, these oils are also available, together with a number of our other products, in the small shop located at the entrance to Coltibuono:

L'Osteria

Badia a Coltibuono, Gaiole in Chianti

Pecorino, Raveggiolo* and *Ricotta

SHEEP'S MILK CHEESE

The streets of the Renaissance town of Pienza are lined with food shops selling *pecorino* cheese and other local dairy products. Allow your senses to be your guide. The following establishments, both situated on Pienza's main street, boast particularly good selections:

Zazzari

Via Rossellino 6, Pienza

Marusco e Maria

Via Rossellino 15, Pienza

In the countryside surrounding Pienza there are also many sheep farms that produce cheese and sell their products directly. These are particularly good places to buy fresh *ricotta* and *raveggiolo* for a picnic lunch. One of these is located along the road between the towns of Pienza and Montepulciano and is called:

Caseificio Silvana Cugusi

Via della Boccia 8, Pienza

Cinta senese

SIENNESE PORK

Butchers in the province of Siena that sell *cinta senese* products will have a sticker on the door of their shop that reads "La Compagnia della Cinta". This association was founded by my local butcher in Gaiole, Vincenzo Chini and his son, Lorenzo, to preserve and promote the *cinta senese*. In their shop you can buy fresh pork and a variety of processed pork products derived from this once endangered Siennese breed.

Macelleria Chini

Via Roma 2, Gaiole in Chianti

Panforte* and *Ricciarelli

SIENNESE SWEETS

Both small- and large-scale bakeries in Siena bake these traditional sweets as well as other local specialities. Try the small, well-respected bakery located on Siena's main street. Easily recognizable, it is a handsome shop with splendid, nineteenth-century chandeliers:

Drogheria Manganelli

Via di Città 71, Siena

Alternatively, try the shop positioned between the Duomo and the Baptistry, where you can watch the bakers hard at work through large windows:

Pasticceria Bini

Via dei Fusari 9, Siena

FLORENCE AND ITS PROVINCE

Trippa fiorentina

FLORENTINE TRIPE

Il Trippaio

Via de' Macci, Florence

(Near the Sant'Ambrogio market.)

Palmiro Pinzauti

Piazza de' Cimatori, Florence

(On a side street between the Duomo and Piazza della Signoria.)

Salame

SALAMI (AND OTHER PORK PRODUCTS)

Antica Macelleria Cecchini

Via XX Luglio 11, Panzano di Chianti

(Ask anyone to point the way.)

Macelleria Falorni

Piazza Matteotti 69, Greve in Chianti

AREZZO AND ITS PROVINCE

Chianina

CHIANINA BEEF

Many of the region's fine butchers sell genuine Chianina beef, should you have a fire to grill it over. Look for a sticker of authorization on the door. Here are two good *trattorie* in Arezzo where you can enjoy an authentic *fiorentina* (a Chianina beef steak). Both are located on the same small street, just a stone's throw away from each other, in the city's ancient historic centre.

Il Saraceno

Via Mazzini 6, Arezzo

L'Agania

Via Mazzini 10, Arezzo

Zolfini

TUSCAN WHITE BEANS

Azienda Agricola Lo Zolfino

Località La Penna, Terranuova Bracciolini

(Located in the province of Arezzo, near Montevarchi.)

Coop Agricola Valdarnese

Località Paterna, Terranuova Bracciolini

(An organic farm cooperative.)

GROSSETO AND ITS PROVINCE

Cinghiale

WILD BOAR

To obtain fresh wild boar meat you need to know a hunter. However, processed pork products made from wild boar are available from many of the region's fine butchers. Try this one in particular:

Salumeria Silvano Mori

Via San Girolamo, Località Torniella

Roccastrada, Grosseto

Anguilla fumata

SMOKED EEL

A cooperative of local fishermen produce and sell this speciality of the Orbetello lagoon, as well as *bottarga*, which is salted roe of grey mullet.

Orbetello Pesca Lugunare

Via Leopardi 9, Orbetello, Grosseto

MASSA-CARRARA, LUCCA, PISTOIA, PRATO AND THEIR PROVINCES

Lardo di Colonnata

COLONNATA LARD

Every producer of this delicacy has his or her secret recipe for achieving the best result. I have never tasted one that was not excellent. The producers of Colonnata lard have formed an association for the protection of their product with some 13 members. Here are two:

Ada Guadagni

Piazza Palestro 4 a–b, Località Colonnata, Carrara

Venanzio Vannucci

Piazza Palestro 3, Località Colonnata, Carrara

Farro

EMMER

This shop in Lucca's historic centre has the best selection of the region's cereals and beans:

Antica Bottega di Prospero

Via Santa Lucia 13, Lucca

Buccellato

SWEET BREAD SPECIALITY FROM LUCCA

Pasticceria Marino Taddeucci

Piazza San Michele 34, Lucca

Brigidini

WAFER BISCUITS

For more than 100 years the Carli family bakery has produced this traditional sweet from the province of Pistoia:

Pasticceria da Pioppino

Piazza Berni 20, Lamporécchio, Pistoia

Biscotti di Prato (Cantucci)

PRATO ALMOND BISCUITS

The best place to buy Prato biscuits is from the bakery where these biscuits were first produced in 1858:

Biscottificio Mattei

Via Ricasoli 20, Prato

LIVORNO, PISA AND THEIR PROVINCES

Pesce

FISH

First visit Livorno's covered food market at the Scali Sassi, then sample the local seafood specialities – *cacciucco* and *baccalà* – at one of this city-port's many good fish eateries. Try Cantina Nardi – a wine bar that serves food – located near the central Piazza Attias:

Cantina Nardi

Via Cambini 6–8, Livorno

Tartufi bianchi

WHITE TRUFFLES

In San Miniato the annual white truffle fair is held every weekend of November. Food stalls with truffles and other local specialities are set up around the town's three main *piazze*. Out of town a good place for purchasing truffles is:

Tartufi Nacci

Via Zara 110, Corazzano

GLOSSARY

UNUSUAL FOODS

beet greens are the green, leafy tops of beetroots (beets). They have dark-green coloured leaves, patterned with rich red veins, and fairly long, upright stalks. They taste a little like spinach and should be prepared in a similar way – steamed, braised, stewed or eaten raw. Alternatively, they can be used as an attractive garnish.

farro (emmer in English) is an ancient form of wheat dating from 7000BCE, and was one of the first staple crops to be cultivated by prehistoric man – traces of *farro* have been found on archeological sites all over the Near East and Europe. It is a tall, low-yielding wheat with small grains and no husk, and is closely related to modern durum wheat, which is used for pasta. *Farro* is sometimes called spelt or starch wheat, and continues to be grown in various parts of Europe today. The grains are commonly used whole in soups, or ground into flour to make bread.

pancetta is an Italian form of bacon (meat from the back of the pig) which has been cured with a mixture of salt and spices but not smoked. It is salty and flavourful, and comes in a sausage-like roll.

polenta is boiled cornmeal. It can be served in its creamy, just-cooked state or allowed to solidify, after which it can be sliced and sautéed, grilled or fried prior to serving. Once seen by Italians as the food of the poor – an inexpensive accompaniment to beans – *polenta* is today regarded as a sophisticated alternative to pasta or rice, and is often served with meat, fish, cheese, vegetables, nuts and sometimes even fruit.

prosciutto is the Italian word for ham, although it is more specifically used to describe a ham that has been seasoned, salt-cured and air-dried. The meat is also pressed, which gives it a firm, dense texture. Italian *prosciutto* is referred to as either *prosciutto cotto* (cooked) or *prosciutto crudo* (raw). Both types can be eaten immediately having been cured, and are usually sold in thin, translucent slices.

rapini (broccoli raab in English) is a green, leafy winter vegetable related to the cabbage and the turnip families. It looks similar to turnip greens (the leafy tops of turnips), with 15–20cm/6–9in stalks and scattered clusters of tiny green broccoli-like buds. Its flavour is slightly bitter – a blend of broccoli, turnip and radish. The Italians are particularly fond of this vegetable, cooking it in a variety of ways, including frying, steaming and braising.

salame **(salami)** is a type of sausage that has been preserved by curing and, in some cases, air-drying; it is therefore eaten uncooked. Salami is usually made from a coarse mixture of pork and beef that has been well-seasoned with herbs, spices and large amounts of garlic.

BASIC PASTA RECIPE

300g/10oz/2½ cups plain flour
3 large eggs
(Serves 6)

Place the flour in a bowl, add the eggs and mix to a dough. Work the dough on a table with the heels of your hands until it is smooth and elastic.

You can use this dough to make any shape of pasta you choose. To make any of the long, thin pasta shapes, it is probably easiest to invest in a manual or automated pasta machine. However, there are many types of pasta that you can make without a machine. To make *pappardelle* (long strips of pasta; see page 77), roll the dough with a rolling pin to form a rectangle, 1mm/$^{1}/_{24}$in thick. Then, cut into strips of about 2.5cm/1in in width.

To cook fresh pasta, place it in boiling, well-salted water for 2 minutes. Drain well, toss with a few drops of olive oil to prevent it sticking, and serve immediately.

ACKNOWLEDGMENTS

AUTHOR'S ACKNOWLEDGMENTS

I would like to thank John Meis for his assistance with the text.

CAPTIONS TO FOREWORD

p.10 A flight of steps leading down to the garden from the main house at Badia a Coltibuono.

p.12 ***(left)*** A view of Badia a Coltibuono from a distance.

p.12 ***(right)*** Copper pans hanging in the kitchen at Badia a Coltibuono.

p.13 The garden walk at Badia a Coltibuono.

CAPTIONS TO CHAPTER OPENERS

p.14 Landscape characteristic of the Crete Senesi near San Quírico d'Órcia in the province of Siena.

p.42 The famous Ponte Vecchio ("Old Bridge"), which spans the Arno River in the city of Florence.

p.68 The tiered portico of the San Francesco colonnade in Arezzo.

p.88 A view from Campagnático of the misty hills of Grosseto at dawn.

p.108 The city of Lucca.

p.132 Fishing boats moored off the coastline of Livorno.